ADVANCE PRAISE

"Phillip Stutts's epic storyline of how presidential campaigns market themselves and the correlation for how this will grow your business is not only a fun read but incredibly impressive. I've now implemented these findings with incredible success into my own business. Simply put, Phillip's Undefeated Marketing System is the real deal."

—JAMES ALTUCHER, SERIAL ENTREPRENEUR, HOST OF *THE JAMES ALTUCHER SHOW,* AND AUTHOR OF *WALL STREET JOURNAL* BESTSELLER *CHOOSE YOURSELF*

"In the last 12 months, everything about marketing has changed. No one understands this better than Phillip Stutts. His vast research into consumer behavior will give you an edge against your competitors and will enable you to win big while they struggle."

—MICHAEL HYATT, *NEW YORK TIMES* BESTSELLING AUTHOR

"With the knowledge and insight that only an insider could offer, Phillip Stutts shows how presidential campaigns can take a country of 330 million people and figure out exactly which few thousand voters in which few states will make or break them—and how to win those voters over. And he makes a compelling case that this methodology has a much wider application than anyone realizes."

—STEVE KORNACKI, NATIONAL POLITICAL CORRESPONDENT, NBC NEWS

"Phillip Stutts has been around over 20 years in the marketing game with Win Big Media—and he does WIN BIG. Phillip knows the inside-out of the marketing game. I've utilized the Undefeated Marketing System's knowledge and techniques to win on the social media front with building my brand. Read this book—it will massively help you too."

—DAVID MELTZER, AUTHOR, SPEAKER, AND ENTREPRENEUR

"I utilized Phillip's Undefeated Marketing System with my brand, and it's helped my business thrive. This book is such an important read if you want to navigate this disruptive world by breaking through the clutter and winning at the game of marketing."

—HEATHER MONAHAN, BESTSELLING AUTHOR AND FOUNDER OF THE *CREATING CONFIDENCE* PODCAST

"If great policy can lead to great politics, then great political campaign ideas can lead to great business marketing success. Phillip Stutts has written the perennial guide for setting your business apart by injecting the world's most powerful political marketing principles into your company."

—DANA PERINO, FORMER WHITE HOUSE PRESS SECRETARY AND COHOST OF *THE FIVE* ON FOX NEWS

"Many marketing strategies that business uses today were invented by presidential campaigns, including data analytics, microtargeting, war rooms, niche blogs, real-time tweets, and much more. Phillip has been at the forefront of pioneering these trends. The entertaining behind-the-scenes stories he tells here also teach how to implement winning marketing in any business."

—DAVID MEERMAN SCOTT, AUTHOR OF *WALL STREET JOURNAL* BESTSELLER *FANOCRACY*

"I'm fascinated by political marketing campaigns and how they can be applied in the business world to produce huge ROIs. The Undefeated Marketing System is a total outlier business book that provides entrepreneurs and marketers with real, actionable solutions for successful marketing. This book is relevant now and will be relevant in 25 years."

—MIKE DILLARD, SERIAL ENTREPRENEUR/INVESTOR
AND HOST OF *THE MIKE DILLARD PODCAST*

To Mike,
Keep growing & follow
this System!

THE
UNDEFEATED
MARKETING SYSTEM

HOW TO GROW YOUR BUSINESS AND BUILD YOUR AUDIENCE
USING THE SECRET FORMULA THAT ELECTS PRESIDENTS

PHILLIP STUTTS

LIONCREST
PUBLISHING

THE UNDEFEATED MARKETING SYSTEM
How to Grow Your Business and Build Your Audience
Using the Secret Formula That Elects Presidents

ISBN   978-1-5445-2016-2 *Hardcover*
       978-1-5445-2015-5 *Paperback*
       978-1-5445-2014-8 *Ebook*
       978-1-5445-2017-9 *Audiobook*

TO ANNIE, MY PARTNER IN THIS WILD JOURNEY

CONTENTS

FOREWORD

I CALLED PHILLIP. HE TOLD ME, "THINGS HAVE CHANGED a lot since last week. Here's what I would focus on if I were you." And then he told me. And it worked. It's like having a super power that tells you what the world is thinking.

This is what Phillip does. It's not a magic formula. But it feels like it.

"This is the most important election ever." I kept hearing that phrase over and over recently. Was it the most important ever? The answer is: maybe.

I went to newspapers.com, which has an archive of every newspaper article in the past 250 years. I searched for "most important election ever."

Guess what?

Every election since 1800 was "the most important election ever."

In 1844, for instance, "The Democratic Party of Perry County... assembled at the commencement of a political campaign which will terminate in one of the most important elections ever held in our country."

In 1868, "Freemen of Vermont! You are called to attend the polls on Tuesday at the most important election ever held in this country."

In 1892, "As all of the speakers have told you, this is surely the most important election ever."

In 1944, "This is the most important election since 1860. It is more than that—it is probably the most important election ever."

Were all of these headlines wrong? No. They really were the most important elections ever. Each election is important to you, me, the candidates, other countries. We aren't thinking about the elections and issues of 1832, or 1844, or 1964. We are thinking about pandemics, wars in the Middle East, our jobs, taxes, and on and on.

Without realizing it, we are also thinking whatever the campaigns want us to think. They are spending billions of dollars to spread a message. To make sure that message is repeated by people on social media or when having casual conversation with their relatives. The campaigns are spending billions of dollars so that people will be convinced that these messages are the only reasonable way to think *or else*...this becomes the most important election ever.

For over 25 years, Phillip Stutts has been on the front lines of using a unique new technique for spreading a message that has impacted tens of millions of people. This technique never existed before. In 1940 it didn't exist. In 1852 it didn't exist. Even in 2000 it didn't exist.

It started in the 2004 US presidential campaign. Phillip spearheaded this new, unique system, and it has gotten more and more sophisticated ever since. Which is why he is among the very first and most experienced to use this system to help businesses. To help even people like me.

Phillip knows more information about you than you think. Not because he spies on you. But because you give your data to many different companies and services. If you read the fine print, you'll see that this data is shared with other companies. And marketing campaigns, led by people like Phillip Stutts, get this data, understand it, and then use it to spread a message.

What information? They know when you will buy your next car, how many strawberries you ate this month, how much exercise you get, what issues your closest family members most care about. Where you are even thinking of vacationing this year.

With that data, they can send 1 message to you, and another message to your cousin, and another completely different message to a customer who lives on the other side of the country.

If this feels manipulative, it is. And it isn't. This is now how every candidate and billion-dollar company does business. This is just the way politics and successful corporate marketing work. And why not hear about the issues, products, or services that are important to me?

During the pandemic and the economic lockdowns, I called Phillip on a regular basis.

"What's new?"

Every week, he was polling thousands of people and getting data on millions more. Phillip is perhaps the first to take the techniques from political campaigns and use them for marketing of...anything. Businesses, political campaigns, even my own personal social media accounts. What do my readers like? What are they looking for?

Businesses listen, I listen, because we want to address concerns that people have. Help people where they need the most help.

Every week, Phillip had his finger on the pulse. Sometimes they were worried about their economic situations. But sometimes they were scared of all the misinformation in the media. Or they wanted to know that their local communities were safe. Sometimes people, as a whole, didn't care about material goods. They just wanted to know if their jobs would come back.

Every week it was different. Every week I called Phillip. Because he knew the answers.

Phillip has been on my podcast close to 10 times. Alongside people like Richard Branson, Mark Cuban, Peter Thiel, Tyra Banks, Danica Patrick, and even Kareem Abdul-Jabbar. Phillip is my go-to guest when I want to really learn what is going on in the world.

Phillip has represented Republicans, Democrats, and now businesses from every industry. What I like is that he is not blindly ideological. He works with data to see what the concerns of the world are and how businesses and political candidates can best meet the needs of the people.

He has helped businesses make hundreds of millions of dollars. He has helped candidates become presidents of the United States. He has helped me and others write good articles for their readers.

In this book, he shows how he does it. I like calling Phillip. But I don't want to call him to do my job. I want to figure out how to do what he does. This is the book I needed to read.

Elections are harsh and dirty and surprising. But let's not forget that many elections in American history have been like that. Let's not forget that in the 1850s, 1 senator almost beat another senator to death in the halls of Congress. Or that John Adams was jailing journalists in 1800 thanks to the Alien and Sedition Acts that he passed and that Thomas Jefferson, in the "most important election ever," swore to overturn.

If elections are going to determine the true representatives of the people, and businesses are going to serve the needs of their customers or clients, we need to determine what those customers, clients, and voters want. What are their concerns?

This can only be done with data. Not opinions. This can only be done if you know how to interpret that data. Not just guess. There are no shortcuts.

Political campaigns started using these techniques as early as...2004...when Phillip started doing it. And now he is doing it for his clients in the business world.

I have to admit I'm lucky. Not only because Phillip is my friend and, in a relatively short amount of time, I feel I can call him and trust him with any issue or problem I'm having. But also because he knows what I should be concerned about, as a business, as a writer, as someone who wants to help people.

It's hard to find someone you trust. It's also hard to find someone who isn't a sucker for all the scripted thoughts inside the echo chambers of social media.

Instead, it's good to find someone to trust who is unbiased. Someone who has mastered using data to make life-changing decisions for elections and businesses. Someone who is willing to share those techniques with us. Someone who is a friend. Phillip Stutts is that guy.

* * *

James Altucher is an entrepreneur and angel investor, having started over 20 companies. He's also the author of the Wall Street Journal bestselling book Choose Yourself *and* Skip the Line *and is founder at the The James Altucher Show.*

ACKNOWLEDGMENTS

I HAVE TO START BY THANKING MY WIFE, ANNIE, AND MY daughter, Parker. Because of you 2, our house is filled with unconditional love, adventure, authenticity, charity...and a bit of chaos. All good things for an abundant and conscious life. I wouldn't be a tenth of the husband, father, and entrepreneur I am today without you 2 amazing women.

I'd be remiss if I didn't shout from the hilltops how grateful I am to my business partner and brother, Dean Petrone. None of this happens without your leadership, friendship, and steady hand. I love you, man.

There are too many friends to thank here, but I want to acknowledge 2 in particular who've been incredibly generous to me and from whom I've learned so much—David Meerman Scott and James Altucher.

David Meerman Scott and I come from opposite sides of the political aisle, yet that never gets in the way of our friendship. David, your heartfelt generosity to engage, listen, and guide is valued beyond the words on this page. It's what one hopes for in a friend. We'd be a stronger country today if more people like you existed.

James, I love everything about you, my friend—but mostly your excitement, kindness, loyalty, and vulnerability. Your friendship is one of the true blessings in my life.

Until I was 40 years old, I was a lost soul and a wannabe entrepreneur—the kind that told people I ran businesses but didn't know what a P&L or balance sheet was (seriously). Then I had an awakening and learned from some incredible business masters. Fortunately for me, some even became friends. I wouldn't be here today if it weren't for these treasures: Tony Robbins, Tim Ferriss, Jay Abraham, Peter Diamandis, Keith Cunningham, Mike Dillard, Darren Hardy, Dave Meltzer, Gary Vaynerchuk, Seth Godin, Mike Hyatt, Bryan Miles, Cody Foster, David Sable, Cal Fussman, Peter Klein, Paul Belair, Steven Gundry, Drew Pinsky, Brad Johnson, Paul Finebaum, Dov Baron, Douglas Burdett, Bill Carmody, Chad Cooper, and Todd Uterstaedt.

To everyone at Win BIG Media and Go BIG Media—thank you for your hard work and dedication to our mission, especially Brent Barksdale, Becca Conti, Carey Cifranic, Andrew Gordon, and Elliot Fuchs.

This book would never have happened had Tucker Max not yelled at me a few years ago to write a book about my business expertise, not one that served my ego. Tucker, you were right, and this book will help so many others because of that shift. To my

Scribe team—Carolyn Purnell, Ellie Cole, and Erin Tyler—your guidance, discipline, and willingness to serve first is something I will never forget. To anyone reading this book that wants to write a great book themselves, Scribe should be your first call.

INTRODUCTION

ON TELEVISION, ELECTION NIGHT ALWAYS LOOKS LIKE A big, happy party for the winning candidate. The victor is all smiles as they celebrate with their family, campaign leaders, and voters. That's because TV loves a happy ending. But let me tell you, for people in George W. Bush's 2004 reelection campaign, most of election night looked nothing like that.

Instead, picture 20 people in a campaign war room hunched over laptops. We were all inches away from our screens, trying to decipher how voter turnout was looking in all the states that could decide the election. Who had actually showed up to vote? What did it look like on the ground? And how were our predictions measuring up?

That kind of tense mood is normal on election night. But when the news website the Drudge Report released its early coverage, things suddenly turned to the jaw-dropping, gut-wrenching kind of tense. Drudge dropped a bomb with an alert that said John Kerry was going to beat President Bush in a landslide.

Even more concerning, their information wasn't based on early voting. It was based on exit polls, which are taken immediately after voters leave their polling places. (Nowadays, we know how inaccurate exit polling actually is. But in 2004, it was the most reliable metric the media used.) Those exit polls were showing that John Kerry was going to rout George W. Bush. In every key state, he was crushing the president, and it looked like it was going to be a bloodbath.

We were completely deflated.

Bush had raised close to $1 billion in a matter of months. We had created the most sophisticated Get Out the Vote operation in history, called the "72-Hour Program" designed to get voters in key swing states to the ballot box in the last 72 hours before the vote. We had worked our assess off, and no one had seen those exit polls coming—least of all me.

I was the national 72-Hour / Get Out the Vote director for the reelection campaign. For 12 nonstop months, I had worked with campaign operatives in the field to figure out what would motivate voters to turn out in the last few days of an election.

Based on everything we had tested and seen in the field, the Drudge Report numbers just didn't add up.

"Stunned" doesn't begin to cover the mood. No one in that war room said a word.

Karl Rove was the first one to act. He immediately jumped on TV and told people to stop talking about the exit polls. "That's not what we're seeing," he said. "We're seeing different numbers. We're seeing record turnouts in places that we expected to have huge turnouts."

Rove was right to try to stop the media in their tracks. Those exit numbers were coming out before all the polling places were closed. They could have easily swayed the election. If Bush voters in battleground states saw those reports, they might have thought, "Well, what does my vote matter if Kerry is just going to trounce Bush anyway?"

"War rooms" have that name for a reason, so come hell or high water, we were going to fight to the last minute of that election. While campaign leaders like Karl Rove went on the media offensive, the rest of us buckled down with our laptops. We trusted our data, no matter what the Drudge Report said.

We were right to stick to our guns. The exit polls were wrong, and President George W. Bush won the 2004 election. Ohio was the key state in the race, and the winning margin was slim. And I mean *slim*. Out of 122,295,345 total votes cast in that election, the race was decided by 118,599 votes in the state of Ohio.

Think about it for a second: *118,599 votes* determined the course of the entire election. Talk about a close race. If only 59,300 votes had flipped from Bush to Kerry, then John Kerry would have won the presidency.

Still, even with all the misinformation, we stayed confident that we were going to win. Why? Because we were following a sophisticated 5-step formula that we knew would carry Bush to victory.

We had unlocked the secret to becoming undefeated.

To understand why this secret formula is so powerful, first you have to understand what made that 2004 campaign so revolutionary. And to really understand 2004, we have to take a step back to the 2000 presidential election.

In 2000, 101,455,899 votes were cast nationwide, and the race was so tight, it hinged entirely on the results in Florida.

Imagine that. The course of the next 4 years was at stake. And it came down to *1 key state*.

Meanwhile, on the ground in that key state, the word "tight" doesn't even begin to describe the situation. Out of the 5,963,110 votes cast in Florida, how many do you think Bush won by?

537.

You read that right: 537—*total*. That's a jaw-droppingly small margin of only 0.0009 of 1%. It was the most disputed presidential race in over 100 years, and maybe of all time.

So, when 2004 rolled around, Bush's campaign manager, Ken Mehlman, did *not* want a repeat. He and Karl Rove decided to do something that had never been done before in American political campaigns. They changed the game with their approach to voter data.

This one innovation changed the course of history and was modeled by every future presidential campaign. Obama, Trump, and Biden all owed their success to this paradigm shift.

Prior to 2004, every political campaign received a "voter file" of data provided by each state. The files didn't reveal who a person voted for, but they allowed political campaigns to gauge who the high-propensity and low-propensity voters were. (We would know if you voted only in presidential years or in every election.) They also included demographic data; we could see ages, ethnicities, how many children were in the household, income level, and similar statistics.

For years, that was it. That was the total voter data campaigns utilized. And every campaign had the exact same information. When the fate of a campaign (read: the fate of an entire country) is in your hands, that's really not a lot to go on.

In 2004, based on Michael Lewis's book *Moneyball* (required reading), our campaign introduced analytics and consumer purchasing data into our decision-making process for the first time. We invested in a brand-new thing called "micro-targeting," which matched that basic voter file with consumer data. Instead of just knowing people's voting tendencies, we had access to thousands of data points on an individual voter: what car they drove, what credit cards they used, what their purchasing behaviors were like, what magazines they subscribed to, and so on.

It may sound simple, but overlaying those statistics changed the entire marketing landscape. We knew, down to the last detail, what made our voters tick.

We knew that certain voters are 1-issue voters. They only show up at the polls when they think their most cherished value is at stake. What we didn't know before micro-targeting was exactly what Jane Doe or John Smith's 1 issue was.

Now we had a crystal-clear perspective on which issues would motivate those voters. We knew who cared about guns, abortion, taxes, education reform, and homeland security.

Then, once we understood what was going to get those voters riled up, we were able to micro-target them with carefully designed mailers, phone calls, and door-to-door visits. Even in an era before social media, we figured out how to speak to them directly about the issues that mattered to them most. The more energized we could get them about their key issue (and our candidate's stance on it), the more likely it was that they would show up at the polls—hopefully with their family and friends in tow.

Since then, data and analytics have become the key to winning elections, and political marketers are extremely savvy about how they use consumer data. In 2008, Barack Obama's campaign took our micro-targeting model and married it with social media, which was just beginning to boom. They did the same in 2012 and far surpassed our 2004 success. Then, in 2016, Donald Trump innovated even further. He combined micro-targeting and social media with branding to create another innovative political campaign. Whether you love him or hate him, everyone knows "MAGA" ("Make America Great Again").

In 2020, Donald Trump got more votes than any presidential candidate in the history of American politics—except for Joe Biden.

Biden won the 2020 election with more than 81 million votes, compared to Trump's 74 million. And do you know how he did it? He and his team used data and analytics to understand what voters wanted.

And what *did* voters want? Voter research showed that people were getting tired of Trump's response to the coronavirus pandemic. They were tired of grandstanding and wanted some peace in the middle of what had been a really turbulent year. In other words, the data showed that the same traits that got Trump elected in 2016 were actually hurting him in 2020.

Trump is who he is. You're not going to change him. So the Biden campaign knew that if they didn't engage with Trump on a daily basis, Trump would eventually dig his own grave with these weary voters. Joe Biden had nothing to gain by going head-to-head with Trump, but he had everything to gain by coming across as a calm, peaceful alternative. So the Biden team ran a stealth underground campaign—which, at some points, seemed like no campaign at all—and clinched a record-breaking win.

The data and analytics methods that were born in 2004 are much more sophisticated now, and they're 1,000 times more powerful. Still, it's safe to say that the 2004 election forever changed political marketing history. In fact, it forever changed marketing history, period—because the very same strategies that put George W. Bush in office can put your business on the map.

After all, politics really isn't that different from business. A candidate is the product you're trying to sell to the voter, aka the customer or client. In both contexts, you're using compelling stories and targeted messaging to convert people.

As you'll see, the "secret formula" that elected every president in the modern age works just as well for the businesses that are willing to implement these steps to grow their bottom line. In this book, I plan to show you the many success stories that you can utilize in your business to win over your customers and clients and grow your business—in any economy.

THE POWER OF POLITICAL MARKETING

The Bush/Kerry election revealed a new, far more powerful way for businesses to connect with their customers and drive conversions. By overlaying your customer/client data with extensive consumer research, you can find out exactly what's going to motivate your customer/client and build a reliable, risk-eliminated marketing strategy around it.

Here's how it works in politics. The first thing I do when I sit down with a political candidate is ask, "What do you believe in, and why do you want to run for office?" Typically, that candidate will give me around 10 policy ideas. *I'm pro-environment. I want to cut taxes. I want to subsidize healthcare. I'm pro-gun rights. I'm pro-choice. I want better education. I want less government regulation. I want to serve. I want to help the homeless. I want higher teacher pay.*

My job is to take those 10 issues, run polls in their district or state, and overlay voter and consumer data to build a deep understanding of what will move voters to such a degree that they'll vote for my candidate. This helps us figure out exactly what voters value. For example, are they more concerned about taxes or the environment? How important are gun rights? Our goal is to find the alignment between what the candidate believes and what will actually get voters to the polls.

We always find that, of the 10 issues the candidate is really passionate about, voters have an especially high level of passion for 2 (or 3). So I tell the candidate, "Those are the 2 issues we're going to talk about. Those 2 high-value issues will make or break the election. Those other 8 issues? We're not talking about them unless we're explicitly asked."

Think about it. When's the last time that you felt jazzed up about a candidate because they constantly talked about 25 different policy issues? Sure, you might appreciate some of those other issues. But for the most part, you're only *really* excited about a handful.

Those are the issues that we're looking for—the ones that move voters solidly into our candidate's column.

Once we've got those nailed down, we design a complete strategic marketing plan around them. We don't want to plan a bunch of whack-a-mole tactics. We need a strategy. So we break our audience into different segments and use research to determine which platforms, media, and messages will spur those voters to action.

We're not looking for slight head nods of approval. We want *enthusiasm and emotion.* We want voters who will fight at all costs to get our candidate into office.

To make that happen, our next step is to tackle messaging, branding, and design. *Every single element* of that messaging is based on our data and the strategic plan. There's no guesswork involved, no toss-it-at-the-wall-and-see-what-sticks. Not when valuable campaign money and time are on the line.

Before we ever spend any ad dollars to send the voter to a candidate's website, we have our brand *nailed down*.

Why?

Because, according to Compuware, 88% of users say that when they have a bad experience on a website, they will never return. Political marketers get that. (As a business owner, do you understand how important this is?)

Once we've got our brand locked and loaded, we take those 2 high-value issues that motivate voters and run tests of those messages 20 to 120 different ways. That way, we can see which ones draw the most attention, clicks, and action. A handful always stand out, and those are the ones we put our weight behind.

How important is it to get this step right?

Pretty damn important when the future of public policy leaders and billions of dollars are at stake. That's why we have to do everything we can to eliminate our candidate's risk.

By following this process, political marketers know we've eliminated 90% of our risk by the time we launch our marketing campaign. We also know, beyond a shadow of a doubt, that our key voters are going to receive messages that motivate them to go to the polls.

Consider that for a second when it comes to your business. Wouldn't you love to know exactly what was going to resonate with your customers *before* you spend most of your marketing dollars? Of course you would. And the 2004 election created the foundation to show us that it's possible.

But here's the thing: *most corporate marketing agencies miss the boat.* They keep doing things the way they've always done them instead of picking up on the massive power of political marketing techniques.

I can't tell you how many times I've heard from frustrated business owners, "My marketing budget is sky-high, but I'm not seeing a reliable return on investment! I never know what's going to work!"

Uncertainty is far too common in corporate marketing. That's because most corporate marketing agencies only play the tactical game. They have a bag of tricks that they use to promote their clients' messages and products, regardless of what the client's needs actually are or what their customers actually want from that product or service.

For example, your marketing agency might tell you that you need "a Facebook strategy." But what if you knew that your customers weren't on Facebook? You could avoid pouring thousands of dollars into a marketing tactic that doesn't have an ice cube's chance in hell of paying off.

The 5-step formula we use in political marketing will tell you right off the bat whether Facebook is a good fit for your customer base. And I will show you exactly how we do it in this book.

We recently worked with a hair care product company that had built a million-dollar business on Instagram. Their owner came to me and said, "We want to expand our operations to Facebook." When I asked why, she said, "Because we've built this company on Instagram, and it feels natural to grow it on Facebook next."

So I asked, "Where are your customers?" She responded, "Well, we assume they're on Facebook."

And there it was. The big A-word. "Assume."

Many corporate marketing agencies rely on assumptions because they know they can make money by playing off business owners' best guesses. If a client comes to the agency and says, "I want some Facebook ads," it's in the agency's financial interest to say, "Sure, how many?" It usually doesn't even cross their mind to say, "Are you even sure that's going to work?"

When we took a deep dive into this hair care company's customer data, we realized that a Facebook campaign wasn't going to get the results they wanted. Facebook was only the fourth-highest-performing social media platform, based on where their customers spent their time online.

We also learned that Instagram, where they had built their million-dollar business, wasn't even the #1 social media platform where her customers actually spent their time. Instead, the top-performing platform for their customers was Pinterest.

This company was about to spend hundreds of thousands—if not millions—of dollars on a tactical guess called "Facebook." And if they had gone to a traditional corporate marketing agency instead of us, they would have done it.

With most corporate marketing agencies, there's a lot of pasta thrown at the wall, and frankly, very little of it sticks. Politics works the other way around. So, before you even boil the water for your marketing pasta, you've got a fully formed plan based on your customer or client data. You have an overall game plan that will work and that also eliminates your risk.

Political marketers are, by far, the most innovative marketers in the world because they have to be. They're always working within a tight deadline called Election Day, and no matter what, they've got to be ready for it.

Not to mention they're also selling ideological messages. Changing someone's mind about gun control or the death penalty is a lot harder than getting a customer to try a new brand of laundry detergent.

My friend Peter Diamandis, the founder and executive chairman of the XPRIZE Foundation, has made the concept of corporate disruption famous, especially in the tech world. But no field is more disrupted than politics. Every 2 years, political marketers have to innovate, test, and persuade voters if they want their candidates to win.

In fact, they don't just *want* their candidates to win; they *need* them to win. Because if a political marketer loses, they don't get hired again. Politics is win or die. If you don't succeed, you're out of business. That's why political marketers are so outcome-oriented. Unlike traditional corporate marketers, they focus every ounce of energy on the success of their candidate. And that's why our formula works.

Maybe you're skeptical. Maybe you're thinking, *Phillip, we're a complicated business. We are B2B, B2C, or e-commerce, and it's not easy to market a company like ours.*

You think marketing a complicated business is hard? Just imagine having to do it for a presidential candidate! I promise, if you can successfully sell a political candidate, you can sell *anything*.

Let's get something straight before we dive in, however. You hate politicians. I get it. But there is a proven marketing system behind getting presidents, governors, US senators, and congressmen and congresswomen elected. And what if you knew that by implementing these secret marketing principles, you would convert more customers and clients in half the time and spend less on your long-term marketing budget? Because you will.

I'm not here to talk politics, left versus right policy issues, or the divisive and corrosive nature of our current political system. I'll leave that for the cable networks. I've worked for a wide range of political clients, from a liberal Black Panther civil rights leader to a conservative Republican president. My personal politics have nothing to do with this book.

I'm only here to help you grow your business faster than a typical tactics-driven corporate marketing firm, which has never faced a marketing campaign where it was a death match between winning and losing.

Every day is a battle to win for me—or I won't be around tomorrow. That's my mindset. I will unlock this secret marketing formula and prove it to you.

BECOMING UNDEFEATED WITH YOUR MARKETING

In 2018, I published my bestselling book *Fire Them Now: The 7 Lies Digital Marketers Sell...and the Truth about Political Strategies That Help Businesses Win*. It was all about how vital and groundbreaking political marketing is, and I explained that every company—B2B, B2C, big, small, *every kind of company*—could transform and amplify their business if they adopted political marketing methods.

At the back of the book, I offered readers a full marketing audit of their company—at no cost. It was the same audit we offer clients at my corporate marketing agency Win BIG Media, which includes a comprehensive and fair assessment of your company's website, social media presence, platforms, and budgets. (This free offer still stands. If you're interested, go to winbigmedia.com.)

Within the first days of the book's publication, I had 35 different business owners take me up on that offer. That showed me that there were plenty of people out there fed up with not knowing how to market their businesses effectively. Who can blame them? After all, Casey Graham, the CEO of Gravy, once told me that for every 44 books on marketing and sales, only 1 is about customer success. *1.*

That's shocking. In this book, I'm going to show you how businesses are succeeding using the Undefeated Marketing System—and explain why.

I've learned since *Fire Them Now* that most business owners don't want to spend money on marketing in the first place, and when they do, they often get taken for a ride by their marketing agency. It's easy to see why that would leave a bitter taste in anyone's mouth.

I've had literally hundreds of business owners tell me that they've already gone through 2 or 3 different marketing agencies, and they're tired of investing all their money into marketing that doesn't work.

So, when I got such a strong response to the free digital marketing "audit" offer in the back of *Fire Them Now*, I thought, "Wow, this is great. People are interested in the idea that there's a different way to run their corporate marketing!"

Not quite.

Of those 35 people, *not 1 of them hired me.*

I was baffled. Why were so many people intrigued but, when push came to shove, unwilling to make the change?

After a lot of soul-searching, I realized that it was my fault. I had explained why political marketing was the best thing since sliced bread, but I hadn't adequately explained what it took to actually adopt political marketing methods—the formula for it.

I'll be honest, these methods feel foreign to a lot of business owners because they're so different from how most corporate marketing agencies operate.

Largely, that's because business owners have an advantage that political marketers don't: time. Most business owners don't feel like they have to move quickly. They have the luxury of talking about their brand "status" or projecting a campaign "into the next quarter."

In politics, speed is everything. Political marketers are working on incredibly short timelines with a specific endpoint: Election Day. If they don't act quickly and win, they're out of a job.

For example, during a recent election for Utah's 4th Congressional District, 2 main candidates went head-to-head: the incumbent, Republican Mia Love, and the challenger, Democrat Ben McAdams. The race was extremely tight. Over a 4 1/2-month campaign, they spent $9 million on their marketing. On Election Day, there were 269,234 total votes cast, and Ben McAdams beat Mia Love by 694 votes.

Think about it. What if you had 4 1/2 months to run a marketing campaign, and at the end, either you or your #1 competitor would be put out of business by a difference of 694 transactions? How fast would you go? How committed would you be to win? Those are the stakes of a typical political campaign.

Want this story to get even crazier? Two years later, Ben McAdams lost his reelection to his opponent Burgess Owens by 3,765 votes, out of 376,701 total votes cast. That's how volatile the political world can be. The sand is always shifting, and any political marketer who can't adapt will be buried by the competition—*fast*.

Business isn't quite so cutthroat, but maybe it should be. What would happen if you changed your perspective? What if you adopted the political marketers' win-or-die mentality?

Don't let your marketing agency settle for a close race. You must do what it takes to win.

This might all sound well and good—and in fact, it did to those 35 "interested" business owners who took my marketing audit. But here's the thing: political marketing strategies aren't for the fainthearted or people looking for a "get-rich-quick pill." They won't work for people who notice a trend and immediately think, *I should have a Facebook ad up tomorrow*, when they don't even know if their customers or clients use Facebook.

The 5-step Undefeated Marketing System isn't for the interested. It's for the committed.

A lot of the clients who read *Fire Them Now* thought, *Great! I like winning! I'm going to give this a try*. They didn't understand that this method requires a system. It takes time. You have to be strict about looking at your customer and client data so you can understand what motivates them. That data has to be your guiding light in all the marketing decisions you're going to make going forward. And I'm going to show you exactly how you can do this, with easy steps along the way.

Those 35 unsuccessful leads taught me a powerful lesson. Business owners need solid proof that these methods work before they'll be willing to follow through.

This book is the proof.

If *Fire Them Now* was my manifesto on why political marketing techniques are the way of the future for corporate marketing, *The Undefeated Marketing System* is my step-by-step guide to implementing those techniques.

This book offers total transparency for my readers. In the wake of *Fire Them Now*, I stepped back and asked myself, What, *exactly*, do we do in politics that is so effective? What are the steps we follow?

I extensively researched every political campaign I had been involved with over the course of my career and studied what had been the key ingredient to over 1,400 wins. I realized that there was an implicit 5-step method every political marketer uses to get winning results.

Notice the word "implicit." No one talks about these steps; it's just the way things are done. But the more I researched, the more I realized that these 5 steps came into play every time a candidate won.

I also realized that almost everything in society follows this 5-step formula. Every sports team, automobile dealer, doctor, trial lawyer, teacher, real estate agent, venture capital firm, golf pro, and hiring process relies on the 5 steps. (I literally could go on for days with industries utilizing this formula.) I'll give you examples from some of those industries in the following chapters. You'll see: they all use it.

Know who doesn't? 99% of corporate marketers.

For the first time, I'm bringing these 5 steps into the open. Not only will I explain what they are, but I'll also show you how you can use this system to get reliable—and impressive—results for your company, in any economy.

If you're committed to the formula, it works every time. You don't have to wrestle with the constant uncertainty of whether your marketing's going to work. And you don't have to blindly trust that your marketing agency knows what it's doing.

Companies that have seen this 5-step method through to the end have all experienced incredible returns. Here are just 5 recent clients we worked with:

- 1 month after their launch (Step 5), an 8-figure national pest control company generated all-time record sales and doubled their conversions.
- After following our 5-step formula, a private educational client has not only seen a steady increase in leads and conversions, but they've also been able to dramatically decrease their per-conversion marketing costs by 41%.
- A New York–based law firm has been able to expand its practice by 8× since undergoing the Undefeated Marketing System.

- A large furniture chain client recently had a 23× return on their Labor Day marketing campaign after following our system.
- A publicly traded product company increased its valuation by $34.8 million after Step 5 of our 6-week campaign.

I've seen it over and over again. The 5 steps work.

With the Undefeated Marketing System, your marketing agency isn't in control. You are. And you're sure to see undefeated growth.

HOW I GOT HERE

I was 26 years old when I was appointed by President George W. Bush to the US Department of Education. I didn't have a background in education, and I had never met the incoming secretary of education, Rod Paige, even though I was going to be his right-hand man. But that's just how Washington works, and I was ready to fly by the seat of my pants and do the best job I could.

A few weeks into the administration, Secretary Paige said to me, "We have to go to the White House for a meeting with the president and some CEOs. We are rolling out our #1 domestic policy priority, which is the No Child Left Behind Act."

Half an hour later, I was sitting in the Roosevelt Room in the West Wing of the White House. Huddled around the table were President Bush, Secretary Paige, and CEOs from some of the country's top companies, like AT&T and Hewlett Packard—and me, this 26-year-old fly on the wall.

The president thanked everyone for coming and got right down to business. "I want to roll out this No Child Left Behind plan to change the American education system, and I want to get your input. How should I market my plan to get support? You guys run companies, and you know how to market."

Sure enough, those CEOs had ideas. They started chipping in and adding their 2 cents.

The whole time, my mind was racing. *This is incredible. This is one of the coolest things I've ever done in my life. But I don't know why I'm here. I'm not supposed to be here.* I had imposter syndrome.

There I was, listening to the titans of business talking about how the president should market his plan to appeal to Republicans, Democrats, Hispanics, African Americans, and every other possible demographic.

It was fascinating.

I had come from the world of political campaigns, and I was no stranger to marketing. But this was my first introduction to seeing just how important marketing really was. The fate of the president's top domestic policy priority was going to come down to how well he could sell it.

I was still reeling when Secretary Paige leaned into my ear and whispered that we were now headed to Nalle Elementary School so the president could read to the kids and take reporters' questions about No Child Left Behind. Not only that, I could check an item off my bucket list: I was going to ride in the presidential motorcade.

At the elementary school, I was on the president's left-hand side the whole time, and thanks to the C-SPAN cameras in the room, that was my first national TV appearance. Everything went smoothly; the kids and reporters filed out of the room, and eventually, Secretary Paige and President Bush left the room, walking side-by-side and talking quietly. I was trailing 3 feet behind them, flanked by Secret Service agents.

This is nuts, I thought. *I'm new to this job, and I already had a meeting in the West Wing of the White House and a ride in the presidential motorcade. Now I'm walking next to the most powerful man in the world.*

The president's voice cut through my reverie, and I heard him say, "Hey, Rod, how's everything going? Are you liking the job?"

Before taking the position in the Department of Education, Paige had served as the superintendent of the Houston Independent School District, and he and President Bush were old friends.

"Yeah, it's going great," Secretary Paige replied. "I'm learning the ropes and trying to figure things out...You know, though, the craziest thing is that, apparently, when you come to DC—no one told me this—but when you get the nomination as a cabinet secretary, they give you one of *these guys*."

He turned around and pointed right at me. The president looked at me and raised his eyebrows. And I thought, *Oh my God.*

In that moment, I realized something that changed my life forever. I realized that DC isn't about money or merit. It's about ego, status, and power.

To someone on the outside, I'm sure I looked pretty powerful right then. I was in my twenties, standing next to the president, after attending a meeting in the West Wing. But in truth, I was an expendable pawn. I thought I was special because I had been appointed by the president. But, in truth, I was just one of "these guys."

Let me be clear. Secretary Paige wasn't trying to be rude. He was being frank. He had a PhD in education, and he had earned his stripes in life. His position in Washington, DC, was the result of a lifetime commitment to education. It was hard for him to believe that there were people like me, appointed solely to whisper in his ear and tell him where he was supposed to go and what he was supposed to do.

That's when I knew I wanted my life to be more meaningful. I wasn't going to be satisfied advising government officials or working in an administration. I didn't just want to work for power or serve myself. I wanted to expand my ideas and help other people.

When I went home that night, I thought to myself, *That was a really cool meeting, hearing about all those marketing ideas. I want to figure out how corporations sell to people.*

Fast-forward to today, and I've spent more than 20 years working as a political and corporate marketing strategist and consultant. I am the founder and CEO of a highly successful political marketing company, and I've been blessed to have contributed to the election victories of more than 1,400 senators, governors, representatives, anyone running—and to 3 winning presidential campaigns.

I've had a colorful career, to say the least. President George H. W. Bush almost threw up on me. I once prayed with and then served communion to President George W. Bush. I accidentally tripped President Gerald Ford and almost killed him, and I worked out with President Barack Obama. President Donald Trump and I took a selfie at the White House, only to realize that we had accidentally excluded the legendary coach Nick Saban, who was standing right next to us. Those are some of the highlights, but the list goes on and on.

In 2017, I partially transitioned away from political marketing and founded Win BIG Media, a corporate marketing company that applies the 5-step formula I learned in the fast-paced political world.

Using the methods you'll hear about in this book, Win BIG Media has helped all kinds of businesses, ranging from small family-owned companies to large Fortune 200 companies and from B2B to B2C to e-commerce. My agency has won a number of prestigious national awards, and I've made more than 350 appearances on national television and media in the last 10 years.

Thanks to Secretary Paige's "these guys" comment and my desire to help others, I spend most of my professional attention on corporate marketing now. But my methods have always been—and will always be—informed by my experience in the world of professional politics.

It was my job to get candidates elected. And I was good at it.

HERE IS WHAT YOU SHOULD EXPECT

Great marketing is like a house. It must be built from the ground up.

This book is your step-by-step guide to creating your marketing dream home. You'll start with the ideas for building (collecting data): What do you want your house to be like? What did you love about your past houses? What worked and what didn't?

With your data in hand, you can hire an architect and start developing your design plan (strategy). What is your house going to look like, how long is it going to take to build, and who's going to do the work for you?

Then you'll buy all the windows, lumber, insulation, and other materials. You'll start pouring the foundation, constructing the walls, and building the roof. Basically, you build the house and start seeing your ideas and design plan come to fruition. That's your brand.

Once your design starts to come to life, inspectors will come in to make sure everything works. You don't want to move into a house before everything is up to code, so this testing phase gives you the chance to optimize your home and make adjustments.

Step 5 (launch) is moving into your dream home. And of course, once you're settled, you'll still have to keep up with routine maintenance.

Each chapter builds on the one before it. We'll focus on each of the 5 steps, as well as some additional challenges that companies encounter after their marketing launch. Throughout each chapter, I will give you an insider account of political campaigns and tell you some incredible corporate marketing stories that will not only entertain you, but also prove why this system works.

At the end of the book, you'll find some low-cost "Tactical Tips" for companies of all sizes, designed to jump-start your returns. All in all, you'll learn how to eliminate risk, create a winning strategy, resonate with your customers or clients, drive them to conversion, and increase your company's bottom line. In a word, you'll learn how to be undefeated.

In Chapter 1, I'll provide an overview of the whole 5-step system and show you how each step works in tandem to create a wildly successful marketing strategy with virtually no risk. You'll also learn why this method is the most effective way to increase your conversions, lower your marketing budget, and give you the greatest ROI your business has seen to date.

Next, I'll focus on Step 1, explaining how customer data insights and research help you determine how your target audience thinks, feels, and acts. Successful marketing isn't about how great your business is; it's about your ability to understand what motivates your customer. When you know what they value, you can deliver. It's also important to go to the media platforms they visit, not just where you want to be.

Using what you know about your target market, Step 2 allows you to build a data-backed marketing strategy that speaks directly to your customers in the most effective way, through the most effective media. Contrary to what your marketing agency may tell you, you might not need to advertise on Instagram. This step will teach you how to build a data-backed plan that will help you stop playing the tactical "whack-a-mole" game and grow your business even more.

Step 3 is where many marketing agencies mistakenly start: developing messaging and creative branding. In this step, you'll see why it's so important to build your brand around your consumer data and according to a strategic marketing plan. If you want to succeed, you have to get your branding right and create content, video, graphics, and websites that resonate to evoke an emotional connection with your customers.

Next, in Step 4, I'll show you how to eliminate most of your marketing risk using data-backed message testing. Starting with a small advertising budget to test various data-backed messages will help you determine which ones most effectively move your customers to conversion.

Once you've got a data-backed message and content that you know works, it's time to launch your full marketing campaign. Step 5 walks you through the launch phase, showing you how to use your laser-focused marketing to drive sales and deliver verifiable growth for your company. I'll teach you how to optimize your marketing's performance, follow changes in the data, and adapt to change day in and day out (because your clients are always changing their habits).

After a marketing campaign is launched, companies will encounter some additional challenges and issues. Chapter 7 introduces you to your most powerful resource for sustaining an undefeated marketing campaign: the retargeting pool. Once a potential customer clicks your ad for the first time, your marketing team must put them into a "retargeting pool" and continually build a relationship with them. Over time, and with a guidebook (your strategic plan), this helps your brand create a loyal community of raving fans. Raving fans are such crazy advocates for your product or service that they'll go out and spend their own capital to give you business, and it won't cost you anything. I will show you how you can easily do this.

Yeti is a great example of a company that has built raving fans. They make coolers, but they've managed to create a raving fan base that buys Yeti brand hats, bumper stickers, and T-shirts. As I write this book, I'm drinking out of a Yeti mug. And now they utilize their marketing dollars to produce amazing entertainment like Yeti-sponsored snowboarding documentaries.

When you break it down, it's kind of a strange idea. Who puts the name of a cooler on a hat and wears it with pride? But that's the power of the brand. They've managed to create such a great product that people go bonkers for them. They've managed to create a horde of raving fans.

In the final chapter, I'll revisit a controversial topic from *Fire Them Now*: "going negative." Contrary to what a lot of business owners think, the most effective marketing allows customers to draw comparisons between your brand and its competitors. People respond strongly when they see your product or service as more effective or more valuable than the competition. This chapter will explain how you can leverage comparative advertising to create even stronger customer loyalty.

Theory is important, but the tools I'm offering in this book are, at their core, extremely practical. In every chapter, I tell practical stories and give examples from both the political and corporate worlds to show you how these steps play out in real-life marketing scenarios. By the time you finish the book, you will see how crucial these 5 steps are for improving your business and driving conversions.

The Undefeated Marketing System isn't always easy.

Actually, I won't undersell it. It is downright hard work.

You'll have to invest some money along the way for research, data, and testing. But the preliminary work you put in will save you hundreds of thousands, if not millions, of dollars. In the next chapter, I'll show you one company that learned this painful lesson the hard way as well.

Think of the Undefeated Marketing System like a course of antibiotics. You can't stop halfway through, even if you think you're healed. If you want your business to thrive, you have to see the method through all the way to the end. You can't chase shiny objects or lose faith partway through.

This book is for the people who want to follow the method that gets presidents elected and grows businesses—every single time.

It isn't for the interested. It's for the committed.

Politicians commit. My clients commit. The losers are just interested until they lose interest.

If you're willing to commit and do whatever it takes to create an undefeated business, buckle up for a fun ride. Let's get started.

CHAPTER 1

THE 5 STEPS OF THE UNDEFEATED MARKETING SYSTEM

IN 2000, I FELT LIKE I HAD THE FATE OF A PRESIDENTIAL election in my hands. To be clear, that's not where it should have been. I was a 25-year-old kid with little marketing experience who was working for George W. Bush's presidential campaign as a political fundraiser. I wasn't exactly "fate of the nation" kind of material.

During the last few weeks of the campaign, it became clear that New Mexico was going to be a battleground target state, so the campaign flew me out to Albuquerque to help mobilize voters. At the time, it seemed like a perfectly logical move. All hands on deck, right? Except that's not what the situation looked like once I was on the ground.

When I walked into campaign headquarters, the guy in charge immediately said, "Hey Phillip, nobody has been doing anything in the southern half of the state of New Mexico. So why don't you get a car and go down to Las Cruces and help us get out the vote?"

Oh, sure. No big deal. I'll be responsible for mobilizing votes across the entire southern half of a key battleground state. No problem.

But we really didn't have another option. I *was* this guy's option. So I moved to Las Cruces and lived out of the Hilton hotel. During the day, I ran a phone bank where volunteers gathered to call undecided voters to tell them they should choose George W. Bush over Al Gore. When I wasn't on-site, I was organizing groups of supporters to knock on the doors of high-propensity voters. We needed to give the campaign a personal touch, and that meant getting face-to-face with as many voters as possible.

Then, 4 days before the election, the media broke a shocking story about George W. Bush. When he was 30 years old, he had been arrested for a DUI.

If you read *Fire Them Now*, you've heard all the gory details about how I learned this information. I was backstage at an event in Las Cruces with the vice presidential nominee, Dick Cheney, and his aide when the news broke, and we all circled around the TV monitors in astonishment. Cheney was just as aghast as everyone else; he hadn't had a clue about the DUI. We knew that all hell was about to break loose.

If New Mexico had been an "all hands on deck" situation, suddenly all those hands were dashing back to DC.

Even though it was mere days before the election and I was in charge of a huge chunk of a battleground state, I went with them. Nobody said a word. At the time, it seemed like a perfectly reasonable thing to do.

Three days later, New Mexico citizens cast 573,200 votes, and George W. Bush lost by a heartbreaking 366.

Of course, Bush still ended up winning the presidency, but it was a nail-biter that came down to a Supreme Court decision because the results were too close to call. I was on the recount team in Florida when the recount finally ended, and I saw firsthand just how slim the margins actually were. They never should have been that close.

States like New Mexico were a big reason why they were. Before that weekend, Bush had a slight lead, but after the news broke and we hightailed it back to Washington, that lead dissolved.

I had left when it mattered most.

That was another defining moment for me. With political campaigns, the most important thing you can do to win over voters is form a personal relationship with them. Knock on their door. Shake their hand. Have a conversation. Maybe my team and I couldn't have found 366 votes in those final 3 days, but damn it, I could have found *something*.

I learned my lesson. I said, "I will never, ever leave any stone unturned. What do I need to do to make sure this never happens again?"

After years of research and experience, here's my answer, and the principle I've staked my entire business on: look at your research to find truth and fact. Find out what people really care about. Figure out what's going to move the needle. Design your approach entirely around that empathetic connection. See what works, and then run with it and see it through until the end.

If we had done that in New Mexico, we might have had a chance at scrounging up the votes Bush needed to win the state. Before the DUI scandal, we were successfully connecting with voters. But when shit hit the fan, I skipped town. I was being reactive instead of following our data-backed strategy all the way to the end.

I'm taking you behind the curtain because I want you to learn from my mistakes. The 5 steps that we abandoned in New Mexico and that could have led Bush to victory there are the same 5 steps that can help you grow your business even more. Let me introduce you to them now.

MEET THE 5 STEPS OF THE UNDEFEATED MARKETING SYSTEM

Even the most successful companies can hit painful roadblocks if their marketing isn't done right. That was the lesson an 8-figure national pest control company learned the hard way.

This 3-decade-plus company had taken a $5 million business to a $20 million one with a single marketing idea. After experiencing a decade of consistent revenue and profit growth, they had even become one of the top pest control companies in America. They thought they were at the top of the world. But suddenly, something changed. Sales flatlined across the board, and they started losing customers.

This is a business owner's worst nightmare. And the worst part? They had no idea what happened or how to fix it.

They had an annual 7-figure marketing budget with a well-known national marketing company, but they still weren't having enough success converting sales. Before long, their competition started eating into the market share, and they watched the value of their company drop from $20 million to $18 million. They were bleeding money from all directions.

Needless to say, they were at their wits' end. And who could blame them? Can you imagine spending *7 figures* a year without seeing returns? Not only that, but spending $1.8 million on their marketing and still seeing valuation *declines*?

That's when they came to me. It was my job to play Sherlock Holmes and figure out why this booming company was now losing out on conversions. By guiding this client through each step in the Undefeated Marketing System, we were not only able to stop the bleeding by identifying what was causing these losses, but we were also able to develop a solution that put them back on the path of steady growth.

STEP 1: TAKE A DEEP DIVE INTO YOUR TARGET MARKET CUSTOMER/CLIENT DATA (3 TO 4 WEEKS)

Every successful marketing campaign is built on a firm understanding of who your customer is, what motivates them, and what they value.

For example, if you're a food product company, you need to know whether your customer base is mostly moms or bachelors. Are they looking for organic food or quick, convenient food? Or somewhere in the middle? Are they more likely to buy in bulk? How much time do they spend online, and are they LinkedIn addicts or Pinterest lovers?

In other words, you need to know who your customer is—and what they value—before you even consider spending your marketing dollars on a bunch of unproven tactics. And there is only one way that a company can truly get to know their customers: by taking a deep dive into customer data.

Let me explain what I mean. If you're a company with thousands of clients, you can't go to each person individually and ask them their name, age, hobbies, what they had for breakfast that morning, how much they spent on their car, what they watched on Netflix last night, and what scent of candle they burned in the bathroom last Tuesday when they were taking a bath. Even if you *could* do that, you shouldn't. It would be downright weird.

Still, if you're a company looking to reach your target market, all that information is indispensable. The fact that your customer regularly buys candles might tell you that they value self-care, or if they regularly buy lavender-scented products, it might suggest that your cleaning products company should consider a lavender-scented line.

The smallest details can still carry a heavyweight marketing punch.

The more information you have on your customer, the more insights you have into what they like and value. This not only benefits your business, but it also benefits your customer. It allows you to develop a stronger, more empathetic connection with them and more directly address their needs.

Actually, this is the problem right now in our society. Most businesses, influencers, and everyone else in the marketing game are screaming "me, me, me." They're not thinking about others. They're thinking about how people can like them. They're thinking about how "popular" they are or how "popular" they want to be. They've got it all backward.

Stop thinking about yourself. Stop talking about yourself. Look at what the customers want and deliver it to them. The most successful marketing is empathetic. It puts the client or customer first.

Just like a political race is mostly about the voter, and less so about the politician, successful corporate marketing is all about the customer or client. You need all that granular information about your customers and clients because that's what's going to help you understand them. That's what's going to help you create more empathetic marketing. And that's what will sell more products and services and make you a pile of cash.

So, if you can't outright ask for it, but you still want to know everything possible about your customer, how do you get that information?

You take a page out of Karl Rove's 2004 election book. In the same way that Karl Rove used micro-targeting to revolutionize political marketing, you can use data and analytics to zero in your corporate marketing efforts.

I'm so convinced that business owners—just like politicians—should be looking at comprehensive data before spending marketing dollars that I formed an exclusive partnership with the largest data collection, analytics, and AI company in the United States. We've got insight on more than 200 million American consumers (trust me, if you're reading this, you're in our database), looking at 550 million–plus connected devices, tracking 10 billion online decisions every day, and monitoring over a trillion searches every day. And that makes our job a zillion times easier and more effective from the get-go.

It may sound obvious, but the more data you can access, the easier it is to know exactly who you're talking to and what your customer or client wants to hear from you about your product or service. Ultimately, marketing to them gets a whole lot easier.

Think of it this way: in politics, you would never market a candidate without knowing what issues voters cared about. Can you imagine marketing a pro-choice candidate to targeted pro-life supporters? It would be an absolute nightmare. Yet I see this happen so often with business owners that it's astonishing.

Why would you market a product or service without having a clear idea of what your customers value?

The right message won't matter if it's not reaching the right audience. You have to understand this from the get-go. Analyzing your consumer data is the only way you can get a firm grasp on your audience's values, motivations, and behaviors.

When I say "data," though, let's be clear. Not all data is created equal.

A lot of corporate marketing agencies rely on generic data, static research, or flat-out assumptions. They run Google Analytics and Facebook Analytics, report their generic findings to the client, and call it a day. Or they look at a survey and decide that a huge, diverse demographic group like "baby boomers" or "millennials" are your target audience.

That kind of data isn't going to cut it for you. There is no way that all 73 million baby boomers are going to agree on *anything*.

When you're analyzing information about your customer, you need to go *deep*. Here's a good example. When we worked for a Fortune 200 company, we segmented their target audience into *over 35 groups*. We looked at males, ages 25 to 30. We looked at females, ages 30 to 32, making less than $30,000, with kids in the household. We got *specific*. When you break your target audience into so many different segments, it gives you a better picture of how people think about your product or service.

You need thorough, reliable, and comprehensive data that tells you *everything* about how your audience lives their lives and what drives them to buy. With better research, you might learn that your company's ideal customer base isn't all baby boomers, but specifically baby boomers who like outdoor activities, buy organic products, and shop at local businesses. You might also learn that they tend to toss mailers straight into the recycling bin, but they respond consistently to digital ads on Facebook. The better your data, the less likely you are to make costly marketing mistakes.

Your first step should always be to compile what I call a Customer Insights Report. This is the culmination of an intensive deep dive into your customer research. The Customer Insights Report pulls together *a lot* of information, and by the time you're done, you'll have a clear picture of everything you need to know about your potential customers. You'll know what media your customers or clients consume, what their daily routines look like, how much time they spend online, why they behave the way they do, and what their personal values are. Essentially, you'll have the low-down on how they think, feel, and act.

You may ask, "Why is this so crucial?" After all, that national pest control company successfully grew a $20 million business without this kind of granular information. Why did they suddenly need it?

Because the data we collected showed *exactly* what they were doing wrong.

When the company came to us, I asked, "What do your customers think?" and they responded, "They like discounts." That was a logical assumption for them to make because the marketing plan (or, more accurately, marketing guess) that had served them well for so long was entirely based around giving customers "discounts."

But the key word there is "assumption." When the company

began using their tactical messaging on discounts, America was in the middle of the Great Recession, so people were looking to cut financial corners.

Even a broken clock is right twice a day, so when their marketing agency settled on a "discount"-based approach, it actually worked for a while. But their luck eventually ran out—like it does with all guesses. The discounts that had served them so well just weren't working anymore, and that's when they started hemorrhaging money and losing market share to their competitors.

A lot had changed over the 10 years since the pest control company developed their original messaging, including their customers' values. So we overlaid their customer list with our consumer database and tracked their online movements for a window of time.

When I dug into their Customer Insights Report, I learned something stunning. The company's target audience was actually *turned off* by discounts. The economy had roared back, and people were making plenty of money. They didn't need to—or want to—buy cheap products. Marketing that repeatedly hammered customers with "discount" messages now felt cheap and untrustworthy to the customer base.

It made complete sense why this company had lost $2 million in market share. They weren't just *missing* their target audience; they were actively *repelling* them. And spending millions of dollars in marketing to do it!

Our Customer Insights Report also shocked the client in other ways. It revealed that, on average, their customer base was retirees with children out of the household. These people had disposable income. They wanted effective service, and many of them placed a premium value on safe, green products that wouldn't harm the environment or their pets.

We also learned that customers' day-to-day decisions were motivated by how to best provide for their family, loved ones, and community. With the kids out of the house, many of these potential customers were putting their time and energy elsewhere. A lot of them volunteered or gave their money to charities, and they valued businesses whose priorities aligned with theirs. It was the trust factor that discounts weren't giving them.

Discounts were the least of these customers' worries. And the pest control company's previous messaging had also missed the boat on both green products and charitable causes—the 2 selling points that could have actually won this group over in spades.

No wonder they were losing out.

By doing what they had always done, this pest control company was *spending marketing dollars to drive away their customer base.*

Think about that for a second. A $20 million company was *paying* to lose business. That's how bad their assumptions were.

Unfortunately, I see this *all the time.* A lot of businesses stumble onto a marketing tactic like discounts, and it seems to work. They throw all their chips on the table, only to figure out later that the success was a fluke. Sound familiar?

Marketing tactics may work in the short term, but unless they're based on a thorough understanding of the customer, they won't hold out. Times change, tactics change, viewpoints change, and your customers' wants and needs change. Unless you know beyond a shadow of a doubt what motivates your customers, you're guessing. And who wants to base their marketing on a guess?

It's your business we're talking about. You put blood, sweat, and tears into it. Eliminate your risk and stop guessing. Luck isn't a stable formula for growth.

By the end of Step 1, your goal is to know what matters to your audience and what will drive them to convert. With this particular client, we found that their customers cared about 3 main things: taking care of their family and community, buying high-quality products and services, and buying green products. Those insights were priceless when it came to developing a marketing campaign that worked.

STEP 2: BUILD YOUR DATA-BACKED STRATEGIC MARKETING PLAN (2 WEEKS)

Marketing seems to change quicker than you can finish this sentence.

The speed of that change makes it easy to get lost in a sea of tactics. One day, Instagram is the go-to platform, and the next day, the news is filled with mentions of TikTok. I've had so many questions from business owners, like "What's better: digital ads or print media? Facebook or Instagram? Banner ads or video?"

These are the wrong questions to ask. It all depends on what motivates your customers and where they put their eyeballs. Your best bet is to be screen agnostic.

Some people respond to social media advertising, while others gravitate toward television ads or even direct mail. Your marketing goal shouldn't be to use as many tactics as possible to reach as many people as possible. It should be to use the *right* tactics to reach the *right* people in the *right* way they want to receive them. (Write that line down!)

If you've followed through on Step 1, you'll already know whether your target customer/client responds better to direct mail, radio, video content, in-app advertising, and so on. You'll know which platforms they use and how they spend their time online.

In fact, Step 1 gave you everything you need to build a solid, data-backed marketing strategy designed to speak directly to your customers. That way, you won't waste money on blind guesses.

Do you think mega-corporations like Coca-Cola toss their money at blind guesses? No way. They spend millions of dollars every year to figure out exactly what will resonate with their customers. When they're building a Christmas ad, I would guarantee you that they even know which customers will be drawn to polar bears, which to penguins, and which to Santa. They know exactly which commuters' eyeballs are going to be on billboards and which moms are watching *It's a Wonderful Life* for the hundredth time.

If a company like Coca-Cola—which, quite frankly, has plenty of ad money to blow if they want to—doesn't leave their marketing campaigns to chance, then should you? Even though you don't have Coca-Cola's marketing budget, you can model their approach. When you see them pivot, pay attention.

But you'd be surprised how many business owners throw money at tactics without having a strategic marketing plan. In fact, Step 2 marks a huge departure between political marketing and traditional corporate marketing. Political marketers use the information they've gathered in Step 1 to create a detailed plan for the entire campaign. What's the *right* strategy to reach the *right* people in the *right* way they want to receive it? (I told you to write that down.)

Meanwhile, most corporate marketing agencies follow the exact same playbook, regardless of the audience or client. If they create some flashy advertisements and run them, they've fulfilled their end of the contract. That's because they're in it for a paycheck, not for your success. They're working for their needs, not their client's, so there's little incentive to develop a strategy specifically tailored to their client's customer.

In political marketing, the client's needs *are* the marketer's needs. A political marketing team could develop the snazziest ads in the world, but if the candidate loses, they will never get hired again. Developing a solid data-backed strategy based on what the voters care about is critical to win an election, which means it's also critical for you to create a marketing campaign that *works*.

The biggest new lie in corporate marketing is that every business should be using digital marketing. But the truth is, there's no 1-size-fits-all marketing solution in today's world.

Your Step 1 customer data will tell you how you should market so you can build an empathetic connection with your customers or clients. That may include digital, but *it may not*. The most effective thing for your business might be face-to-face marketing or print media. It might involve radio ads or attending local events. I'll say it again: *there's no 1-size-fits-all marketing solution*.

If your marketing agency tells you there is, fire them now. They're leading you down the road to defeat. And you deserve better. Your customers deserve better too.

Let's get something straight. Customers often buy products or services because they want their needs met, not because you roused their curiosity with a cute ad. In the case of our pest control company, we knew that 99% of people's number 1 objective was "I need my bugs killed." Point-blank.

When you want your bugs to die, what do you do? You go to Google and look up "pest control company." Or "pest control in my area." A list of 30-ish companies will pop up, and typically, people will pick the top 2 or 3 to research. Our client paid for a high ranking, so we didn't have to do anything special at that point to catch a customer's attention.

But once a customer clicked on those 2 or 3 sites to comparison shop, guess what? Every competitor was saying the same thing: "We kill bugs." Great. But what about that makes them distinctive? What was going to make a customer hire our client, instead of the 2 other top bug-killers?

We had to figure out how to make our client stand out. *We needed to find the difference that made the difference.*

That's when the 3 Customer Insights Report takeaways from Step 1 became so important. We knew that our client's customers valued family and community, and they weren't as willing to trust an impersonal company or national chain. Based on that information, we were able to develop a marketing strategy that spoke directly to those values.

Our pest control client was a 35-year-old family-owned business that had been passed down through 2 generations. They had regularly contributed to local community charitable causes, but here's a shocking fact: the company had never told that story within their marketing to get new customers!

They were already doing everything their clients wanted, but they weren't capitalizing on it! All because they had skipped Step 1 and based their marketing on a bucket of bad assumptions. We knew right away that the company's community involvement would set them light-years apart from their competitors. We also knew that trust and safety meant everything to this company's target audience, so we focused our strategic plan on ways to reorient the brand around green products.

Finally, we built a plan that addressed the customers' financial values. The Customer Insights Report had clued us in to the fact that these customers distrusted "discounts," but guess what? They loved "bundling" services. Their phones, cable packages, streaming services—these customers were bundling all over the place!

Discounts made them feel the service was cheap, but bundling made them feel like they were smart and effective with their choices. They could be penny-wise without compromising on their high standards. So our strategic plan was all about bundles. For example, clients could buy a package that included quarterly pest control and annual termite service.

I want to emphasize something. In politics, the goal of a strategic plan isn't to change a candidate's values. If your candidate supports the Green New Deal, you're setting yourself up for a world of hurt if you try to push a pro-oil-and-gas strategic plan. Not only will your candidate balk, but voters will see right through that inauthenticity. The goal of a strategic plan is to highlight the 2 or 3 values your candidate already *believes* that you know will make the biggest difference to voters.

Likewise, your company's strategic marketing plan isn't about changing your company. It's about bringing the things you're already doing more into alignment with what your customers want from you. We weren't trying to convince these customers that they were wrong about discounts or that green products are for suckers. Instead, we looked for ways that the customers' values meshed with what our client was already doing.

I'd also like to point out that already—by Step 2 of the Undefeated Marketing System—we had eliminated all the guesswork that had been draining this pest control company's coffers. We had also eliminated a huge chunk of their marketing risk and established a clear path to successful messaging—all because we focused on what the data told us about our client's target audience and then built a strategic plan around it.

When you bring these steps into the open, nothing seems more obvious. *Of course* you want to connect with your customers. *Of course* you want to focus on a strategy that will reach them in the most effective ways.

But I can't tell you how rare this "obvious" approach is in the marketing world—and how revolutionary it is for your company's continued success.

STEP 3: CREATE YOUR DATA-BACKED MESSAGING AND CREATIVE BRAND (OR REBRAND) (2 TO 4 WEEKS)

If you live in Florida and want to get to New York, would you book a flight that takes off from Washington, DC?

Of course not. Starting a journey in the middle is pointless. At worst, you'll never get where you're going, and at best, it will open you up to all kinds of headaches.

That's why I find it so galling that a lot of corporate marketing agencies start their client campaigns with Step 3. They push the need for branding (or rebranding) as a way to score a huge advertising budget. They jump straight into creating website content, videos, and graphics that cement who your business is and what you do—but it's rarely based on the message your customers want to hear.

Unfortunately, corporate marketing agencies are incentivized to create advertisements around their client's brand *before* considering what motivates their customers or where there is alignment between the 2.

That would never fly in a political campaign. Can you imagine building a series of campaign marketing ads without knowing what voters cared about? A fancy video on your website isn't going to get you very far if your candidate can't connect with constituents.

When marketing agencies do this, they're thinking about a brand, not a business. And unfortunately, that's also when they hit serious roadblocks.

There's no better example than the sports industry during the coronavirus pandemic. In June of 2020, we ran a Customer Insights report that analyzed more than 200,000 consumer surveys and matched the results to over 200 million consumers. I knew they were in deep shit.

Eighty percent of American sports consumers didn't want to attend a live event until there was a coronavirus vaccine. It's pretty damn hard to run sporting events when leagues enforce social distancing policies and a huge segment of the customer base (fans) decides not to attend.

Now add in the simultaneous Black Lives Matter protests that were taking place during that time, and you had a double whammy for sports brands. Our Customer Insights Report showed that the vast majority of sports fans weren't "woke," and they didn't want a team, player, or brand to inauthentically preach to them about social values. Oh, I know you want to cancel me for saying that, but the data clearly showed that 87% to 92% of Americans didn't want to hear about wokeness from corporations or Gen Z athletes.

Meanwhile, brands like the NFL, NBA, NHL, and Major League

Baseball kept promoting their political agenda in their messaging, and their ratings plummeted. It was because they didn't match their messages to their customers' values.

The only brands that could successfully turn social justice messaging to their advantage were brands like Nike and Patagonia, who had been on the frontlines of these causes for years, far before inequality or police brutality were in the headlines.

If you don't base your branding on customer insights data, you risk alienating your audience. Or worse, pissing them off. Content creation and branding should *never* happen until you've got a firm grip on who your customers are, what they want, how you're going to reach them, and how that aligns with your outcome and vision.

Every bit of creative content that we created for our pest control client was based on what we found in the Customer Insights Report. *Every. Single. Bit.*

We redesigned their website to showcase their new bundling options. We created digital and video ads that stressed their use of environmentally friendly products. We even helped rewrite the sales team's phone call scripts to make sure that the company's local, community-minded values came through.

Every action aligned with our customer insights and evoked an emotional connection with our client's target audience. For example, we created a humorous video ad that showed people in a variety of irritating situations: spilling coffee on an important report, being stuck in gridlocked traffic, and a wife tossing and turning next to her snoring husband.

A dramatic voice announced, "We can't get rid of all the things that pester you, but we *can* get rid of all your mosquitos and other pests...As far as the other pests? Well, then, you're on your own." The video showed uniformed, highly trained service providers, while the voice-over emphasized that the company is "local," "effective," and "safe." In 15 seconds, we managed to draw viewers into an emotion and then deliver a message that we knew would resonate with their values.

Did it work?

Our client saw a 235% increase in monthly phone calls and had 3 times more monthly sales conversions. So, what do you think?

STEP 4: TEST YOUR DATA-BACKED MESSAGING TO PROVE WHAT WILL WORK (4 TO 6 WEEKS)

You now know your customer inside and out. You have a game plan. You have a brand that you know will work when the customer is ready to shop. It's go time, right?

Wrong.

There's one more step you have to follow before you're ready to launch your new, low-risk marketing campaign: message and ad testing.

But Phillip, why do I need to test my messaging if I know it's supported by my research?

Great question. Every message you developed during Step 3 will work, you're right, but it's inevitable that some of them will work better than others when running ad campaigns. And it's worth taking a few extra weeks to figure out which ones are going to send your sales through the stratosphere.

Trust me, your bottom line will thank you.

Now, when I say "testing," I don't mean that you need to go all-in. Start with a small advertising budget and test various data-backed messages. The point here is to save the majority of your marketing budget for launching your most successful content in Step 5.

For example, one of our clients was a previously B2B-only retail clothing company. They had been successful in generating sales through major licensing agreements with sports and entertainment outlets, including the NBA and NHL, but they hadn't been able to leverage that success into a direct-to-consumer marketplace. People were raving about the shirts of their favorite teams and musicians, but they had no clue which company was actually making them.

It was our job to change that.

After working through the first 4 steps with this client, we had developed a strategy and content based on what we knew: the data clearly said this client's customers needed to feel status and significance. They were willing to pay a premium for clothes that made them feel important—but before they were willing to open their wallets, they had to know, without a doubt, that they were buying high-quality products.

That messaging—high-status, high-quality, and high-profile—was locked and loaded. We knew it would work. What we didn't know was which specific angle would show the best results. So we ran a series of 10 ads with different message types supported by our research. For example, we ran ads featuring real 5-star reviews from other customers, comparative "negative" ads focusing on big-brand competitors, and ads featuring celebrities wearing the products.

All of them worked, but a few of them *worked*. The ads that blew through the roof with women were "social proof" ads with the 5-star reviews. The ads that performed best with men were our comparison "negative" ads, where we took a shot at a bigger sports apparel company.

When our client ran those ads, customers spent almost *double* the amount on their first purchases than they had before.

A lot of marketing agencies run high-cost tests and hope for the best. They spend a huge chunk of the budget on ads that may not work, without considering the client's needs. From the marketing agency's perspective, if it doesn't work out, they always have more creative ideas waiting in the wings, and they know that many business owners will just keep footing the bill.

Political marketers know better. Testing is a tried-and-true part of our playbook. Before launching a full marketing campaign, political marketers typically test dozens of slightly different ads to see which ones get traction.

It's a genius move because it allows you to see which messages will most effectively advance your customers to conversion—and to do it at a very low cost. You're able to constantly evaluate your ROI at scale, without wasting a lot of money on messages that don't work. In other words, the first 3 steps give you the cream of the crop, and Step 4 helps you find the most perfect drop of cream imaginable.

Our pest control client saw the power of this "cream" firsthand when we ran a series of low-cost ad tests. Our graphic designer and video production team created 10 different ads with 10 different messages, and we spent 6 weeks tracking them all to see which ones people clicked.

Once we knew which ones blew the others out of the water, those were the ones that we went all-in on for the launch.

Here's the reason I say that the Undefeated Marketing System is for the *committed*, not the interested. By the time we got to the end of Step 4, our pest control client had spent $35,000 to $40,000, and they still hadn't launched their marketing campaign. (Remember, this was an 8-figure company, and they wanted to spend this money to get it right.)

That's a lot of money, but let's put it into perspective. Before this company realized that they needed to find out what their customers wanted—not just what they *assumed* their customers wanted—they had lost $2 million of market share and wasted $1.8 million in marketing costs.

What's more expensive?

I get it. When your business is losing money (or earning money more slowly than you'd like), it's hard to be patient. I can't tell you how many times I had to remind myself to slow down and cool my jets when I was working in the lightning-speed world of political marketing.

A lot of companies get antsy during the testing stage. They've spent time and money on data, a strategic plan, and branding, and they're eager to push their campaign out into the world and start making money.

Don't give in to that temptation. Time is of the essence, but I promise you, Step 4 is worth the wait. It's where to find the gold.

In addition, it's absolutely crucial because Step 4 is where you eliminate even more of your risk. By the time our pest control client was ready to launch their campaign (Step 5), they had a message that was virtually guaranteed to work. They knew they were going to be undefeated. Isn't that worth a little bit more time?

STEP 5: LAUNCH YOUR DATA-BASED MARKETING CAMPAIGN (ONGOING)

Once you've come back with some conclusive "wins" from the testing phase, you are ready to finally launch the full marketing campaign. By now, your marketing efforts will be laser-focused, and you'll be using only the highest-ROI messages and content.

You're primed to win.

Still, let me be frank. Your launch isn't a 1-time event. You'll need to constantly evaluate your results and customer data, and periodically revisit the other steps to see if you can improve and optimize your ROI.

Remember, messaging around discounts worked for our pest control client for almost 10 years before they suddenly stopped working. Marketing is always evolving, and so should your strategy.

But here's the good news. Because you've got the other 4 steps under your belt, ongoing adaptation will be much easier. You won't have to reinvent the wheel every time you want to improve your message.

So, how did the Undefeated Marketing System work out for our pest control client?

After following the 5-step formula, they had the all-time highest monthly sales record in their 35-year history. Within 9 months of working with us, they had completely turned the boat around. They reversed their customer loss trends and saw nearly 2 times more total conversions. Since then, they've consistently grown their client base, month over month.

The system worked, they are still our client, and now they're back at the top of their field.

WHY THE FORMULA WILL WORK FOR YOU AND WHERE ELSE YOU CAN SEE THE STEPS IN ACTION

Most business owners are proud of the businesses they built.

They should be! They've taken on debt, worked long hours, and taken risks without knowing whether they can produce outcomes. They've put their families and financial futures on the line for an idea they believe in. I get it!

Because they're so fully immersed in the companies they've created, most business owners have gotten really good at telling their story. They can tell you everything about how the business started, how it grew, and what it can do. Does this sound like you or your boss?

What they often forget is that their customers aren't always interested in that story.

I'm going to level with you. Almost no one cares about your business except you. Your customers care about how your business can meet their needs. They want goods and services that will make their lives easier, better, nicer, or more efficient. If you're a huge success along the way, so much the better. But your success will never be a real concern for your customer. Seriously, how many times have you watched an ad and thought, *Wow, that CEO deserves to make more money?*

Business owners and marketers need to learn to separate their business's story from the stories that customers care about. And let me be clear, this isn't an indictment. I do the exact same thing. I mix my stories all the time. It's just how we business owners are wired.

That's okay. After all, that's why you hire a marketing agency—to help you figure out what stories *will* matter to customers.

But here's the problem. Too many marketing agencies prey on the business owner's ego. They tell the owner, "You've got the greatest business," and they spend massive amounts of money creating a brand that focuses entirely on the business's or the owner's "story."

Ads don't work when customers hear "Our business is very successful." They work when customers see them and think, *Wow, I need that.* Or *Wow, that service will help make my life easier.* Or *Wow, buying that product is something I need, and it will also let me contribute to a cause I care about.*

That's why the 5-step formula is so powerful. It works because it puts the customer back at the center of your marketing. It forces you to shift your marketing focus away from your business and to look at what motivates your customer.

That's also why it works for political candidates. By the end of an election, a successful candidate has a raving fan base that's willing to vote for them at all costs. But 99% of them didn't get there because they said, "I'm the best." (Okay, maybe Trump did this, but he's the outlier 1%.) They got there because they focused on the issues voters cared about. They spoke voters' language and put their needs front and center.

This 5-step formula also works in almost every other social context. Once you start noticing it, you'll see it everywhere. Seriously. *Everywhere.*

I'll give you tons of examples throughout the book, but for now, I'll zoom in on a few other areas and give you a better picture of why this secret formula works every time.

I have achalasia, a rare esophageal disease where the muscles and nerves that contract food to the stomach don't work. They're dead. I've had 18 minor procedures, 3 major surgeries, and 2 experimental clinical trials so far.

Doctors told me the cause is unknown, but I assume it was caused by an autoimmune response to a lifetime of stress and eating the wrong diet. When I read Dr. Steven Gundry's *New York Times* bestselling book *The Plant Paradox*, I realized just how wrong my diet really was.

Not only did I decide to take matters into my own hands and cure my disease, but I also decided to change my diet with the outcome of eliminating all prescription medications for the rest of my life.

That's right. I have a disease without a known cure (yet), but I wanted to eliminate all of my prescribed medications.

And here's the crazy thing: the 5-step formula that elects presidents and markets businesses is the same formula Dr. Gundry uses to treat his patients and put them on a path to abundant health.

Dr. Gundry's first step was to evaluate my medical data. Initially, he took 18 different blood samples and classified 127 different indicators into 3 groups: positive (above average in a good way), neutral, and dangerous.

His second step was to create a strategic plan for my goal of getting off all prescription medications. With my blood data and goals in hand, we created a health plan that requires me to follow the Plant Paradox diet and increase my supplement intake where I had major deficiencies. For example, if I have too many lectins—the proteins that make plants hard to digest—in my diet, I can take a natural, organic supplement that offsets their effects.

In the same way that a disorganized website says something negative about your business, a dysfunctional body says something about your health. That's where Step 3—rebranding—comes in. Your body is your brand, and if you don't feel great, you won't be great. Dr. Gundry taught me to focus on working out, getting sufficient sleep, and using yoga to improve my mental health and stress. The "messaging" in our rebrand speaks directly to my needs, and let me tell you, I have never felt better in my life.

During the "testing" phase, Dr. Gundry recommended that I take 40-plus supplements a day to combat the "dangerous" blood test results and improve my "average" results. After 6 months of proper diet and supplement intake, Dr. Gundry conducted all the same blood tests again. We looked at where I had improved and where the supplements didn't work.

Finally, we had a complete and total understanding of my body, what it lacked, what it needed, and how it should be fed. By the time we were ready to "launch," Dr. Gundry was 100% sure about what would work.

The results? Today, I take *zero* prescription medications for what doctors call an "incurable" disease. I now take 53 supplements per day to maintain a healthy life, and I still follow the Gundry diet with the foods I eat. All the vitals in my body are in either the positive or neutral zone, and every single test result has moved in the right direction. According to the data, I'm the healthiest I've ever been in my life.

Whether you apply it to your health or your business, the 5-step formula works.

THE 5-STEP FORMULA IN SPORTS

What's the difference between a political campaign and football season?

It's not a riddle. In fact, it's not even a real question because the fact of the matter is, there is no difference. Just like politicians, all sports teams follow this 5-step undefeated formula. They're in constant competition. They're forced to constantly innovate. And there's a hard deadline for victory.

Just think about it. Every time a football team meets to watch footage from last week's game, they're gathering data. Coaches work behind the scenes to learn their future opponents' go-to plays, study specific opponents' strengths and weaknesses, and hunt for hidden patterns in their team's wins and losses. This is all data evaluation. That's Step 1 to a T.

Then, using that information, they come up with a game plan. They build a weekly playbook, discuss ways they can exploit their opponent's weaknesses, and come up with strategies for winning the upcoming game. The emphasis here is on the word "strategy."

No sports team goes into a game without a clear strategic plan for victory. Winning teams don't leave anything to chance any more than winning politicians do. When a team has a better strategy than their opponent, it shows.

Step 3—branding—has nothing to do with the players, but it's still essential for any team that wants to get fans to buy tickets. Do you want to attend a game that has trash left over from the previous week or where the team brand isn't painted in the end zone? No way. The stadium gets a thorough cleaning. Someone washes the jerseys of every player to make sure everything is pristine and ready to go before game time. The brand has to be on point if they want a full house each week.

Every practice is a Step 4 testing ground. Players practice plays over and over each day. They learn to anticipate what their opponents are going to do, and they use practice to devise ways to thwart them. Practice is where they eliminate more of their risk and prepare themselves to become unstoppable.

You cannot be an undefeated team or a playoff team without daily discipline. The same goes for your marketing. You can't skip the steps, and you can't go undefeated unless you're getting into shape months before the first game. Winning takes preparation. But that preparation will always pay off.

Then, when the football team enters the field to play the game, that's the final step—launch (Step 5). Now that they've figured out which plays will work and which ones won't, and they've practiced all week long, it's time to put those steps into action. But remember, a successful launch is ongoing. Players and coaches need to make constant in-game adjustments, based on all the feedback they're getting during the game.

The team that masters these 5 steps best will be the winner.

THE 5-STEP FORMULA TO GETTING MARRIED (SERIOUSLY)

Like I said, once you start noticing the 5 steps, you'll find them everywhere. I wasn't kidding. They're even an essential part of romance. Check this out:

Step 1: You do your research by going on lots of dates and figuring out what you like and don't like. You'll make lots of mistakes, think about the ones that got away, and question your decisions. Even if you're not aware of it, you're storing every piece of data for the future.

Step 2: As you get more serious in finding a life partner, you create a game plan for what you want. What are your nonnegotiables? Does the other person want kids? Are they willing to move around a lot, or are they committed to living near family? Does it matter if they're hurricane-level messy? Answering all these questions about your goals and desires is a necessary part of coming up with a strategy to find a lifelong partner.

Step 3: Before you go on a date, you're branding yourself. You work out, dress nicely, and present yourself in the best possible light. When you're on the market for a potential partner, you're always looking to put your best foot forward. You wonder, *How will that person see me?*

Step 4: As you keep going on dates, you're testing out what the data suggested might work for you. After going on 2 terrible dates from some dating app, you might not want to try that again...If you did find someone who ticked all the boxes, you ask yourself whether there's something you missed. You keep dating that person until you're confident you could spend the rest of your life with them.

Step 5: Once you've found "the one," it's time to launch. Get married; start a family; be happy!

Of course, you're far from done once you get to Step 5. You'll have to keep going back to the data, time and time again. You'll make compromises, adjust your strategy, and, yes, over time, you might even have to tweak your brand and test some new messages (or you'll get divorced). A launch is never a one-and-done situation, whether you're talking about marketing or marriage.

DON'T LEAVE STONES UNTURNED

The 5-step formula is all around us, but for some reason, 99% of marketers don't follow the steps. The companies that have risen to the top of the pack are the exceptions to the rule.

Think about it. Why have 4 or 5 tech companies become the biggest in the world? All of them made an important realization: they aren't e-commerce companies or search engine companies or social media companies. First and foremost, they're data companies.

That data allowed them to tap into the secret formula to accelerate their business's growth. Data helped them learn how you think, feel, and act, so they were able to deliver ads and marketing that spoke directly to their customers.

Are you doing this? Or are you telling people how great your product or service is without figuring out what motivates your customer?

Back in 2000, political marketers hadn't tapped into the 5 steps yet. Data analytics was still a glimmer on the horizon, and we weren't as savvy as we could have been about what would motivate voters to turn out for George W. Bush.

Of course, there are any number of things that went wrong in New Mexico. It would be easy to blame George W. Bush for hiding his DUI, grumble about the fact that the media picked up on it right before Election Day, or scoff at the fact that no one was really active in southern New Mexico before my feet hit the ground.

But here's the plain and simple truth: we didn't have the data we needed, and we didn't stick to a plan. Instead, we followed our instincts and made wild guesses, and that led us to make some significant mistakes. We left stones unturned because we thought we already had our bases covered, and it came back to bite us in the ass. That was decades ago too.

You should never market a political candidate without knowing how to align their values and policy positions with the voters. The same applies in business—never market your company without knowing what matters to your customers. And to know that, you have to do some legwork before launching. You have to research, build a strategy, brand (or rebrand), and test.

If you start applying these 5 steps—not just to your marketing, but to your life in general—you will have a monster edge. Don't leave stones unturned, and stop leaving money on the table. Rely on the data if you want to be undefeated.

CHAPTER 2

STEP 1: TAKE A DEEP DIVE INTO YOUR TARGET MARKET CUSTOMER/ CLIENT DATA

THE REPUBLICAN PRIMARIES FOR THE 2016 PRESIDENTIAL election were packed. In fact, there were more candidates running than in any other presidential primary ever. But by the end of 2015, the field had narrowed to only a handful of candidates, and in Iowa, 2 candidates were clearly in the lead: Donald Trump and Ted Cruz.

I was working for a super PAC representing Ted Cruz in the Iowa caucus race. (A super PAC is a political action committee that can advocate on a political candidate's behalf.) In the run-up to the February 1 voting day, the numbers were showing that this race was going to be a squeaker. If we wanted Cruz to win, we had to follow the 5 steps—and follow them fast. We had to find the ammunition that would *bury* Donald Trump in Iowa and push Cruz to victory.

A few days before voting began, Des Moines hosted the seventh primary debate, and we knew the hot-button issues that were going to come up: the water crisis in Flint, Michigan, whether police officers should wear body cameras, and the ever-present question of healthcare reform.

But behind the scenes, the real question was how Cruz could put the nail in Donald Trump's coffin in this critical first caucus race. The debate was one of Cruz's last chances to clinch the vote with undecided Iowa caucus-goers. The stakes couldn't have been higher.

How could Ted Cruz show Iowa voters not just that he understood the ins-and-outs of these issues, but that he also, on a deep level, *got them*?

If policy nudges people toward the polls, enthusiasm shoves them directly to the voting booth and pulls the curtain. These voters needed to be motivated. They needed to feel passionate about Cruz. In a word, they needed *fire*.

Then, with less than 150 hours before the voting started, Ted Cruz got the perfect pre-election gift: Donald Trump pulled out of the debate. Trump claimed that Fox News, one of the debate sponsors, had treated him unfairly. He made the risky bet that pulling out would bring him more coverage—and sympathy—than being onstage.

What Trump didn't anticipate was just how ready Ted Cruz was to hit that stage with guns blazing. And without Trump there to suck all the oxygen out of the debate, Cruz managed to run the stage.

During the debate, Cruz told 12.5 million viewers: "[Trump] said, 'Look, I'm from New York. Those aren't Iowa values, but this is what we believe in New York.' And I guess I can frame it another way...Not a lot of conservatives come out of Manhattan."

It wasn't his only zinger of the night, but it was a solid blow to Donald Trump's otherwise impenetrable armor in the state. Cruz's reputation told Iowans, *I see you. I know what you care about. And that guy doesn't even like you or where you live!*

The Cruz campaign's strategy had worked. He was far from a shoo-in, but he had made some headway. His no-nonsense words got the attention of Iowa Republicans.

Now it was our job to make sure that Ted Cruz didn't sink back into the pack. We needed to take his words and keep the fire burning. We asked ourselves, *What can we do to convince caucus-goers that Cruz is the man for the job? What's going to be the difference that makes the difference?*

When we dug deep into our Iowa caucus voter data, we learned that Republican voters in the state only had one reservation about Donald Trump: he was from New York, so he represented New York values.

That resonated perfectly with what we had seen in the debates. When Cruz took a stand against Trump's New York values, voters paid attention. How could a guy from the Big Apple understand what it was like to live in the Hawkeye State?

Our research revealed that Donald Trump's Achilles' heel with

Iowa voters was his big-city lifestyle, and we also knew Iowa caucus-goers were pro-life voters. So we went on a deep dive. And when I say deep, I mean *deep*. This wasn't a "google it and you're done" kind of a situation.

Do you know what happens when you dig into political campaigns? Eventually, you strike gold. We managed to find an old clip of Donald Trump that was sure to scandalize any Iowa voter still straddling the Cruz-Trump fence.

In an old interview with NBC News, Trump had said, "I'm very pro-choice, and again, it may be a little bit of a New York background. I lived in Manhattan and New York City all my life, so you, know, my views are a little bit different than if I lived in Iowa."

Bingo.

We had the right data, we knew the strategy, and we knew how to brand the ad. We tested it online, and it crushed, so we launched it. We created a 30-second ad that juxtaposed Trump's "New York" moment and Cruz's debate smackdown. We called it #CruzMicDrop and aired it all across Iowa.

Cruz ended up winning the Iowa caucuses with 27.6% of the vote, versus Trump's 24.3%. And our ad ended up winning a Pollie Award for "Best Internet Ad for a Presidential Campaign."

There are 1,000 victors in a race like this. Everyone says that what they did was the thing that won the race, when really, it was probably a lot of things. But I will say this: our ad was enormously effective, and its results were exactly what our data and research indicated.

Just like political marketing, the first step of successful corporate marketing is to figure out how your target customer or client thinks, feels, and acts. If you don't know what makes them tune in or turn off, there's no way you're going to catch their attention. And the only way to know that with any degree of certainty is to gain a deeper understanding of them so all your branding, sales copy, ads, marketing—and ultimately, your products or services—resonate.

IF YOU ARE STATUS QUO, YOU'LL BE DEAD SOON

Let me give you some shocking figures.

According to Singularity University, in the mid-2010s, there were 500 million internet-connected devices. In 2019, there were 35 billion. By 2030, there will be *1 trillion.*

Every day, the average person scrolls through *300 feet* of mobile content. That's the same height as the Statue of Liberty or Big Ben.

According to *Forbes*, that same person sees up to *10,000* online and offline ads daily.

Let me repeat that. *We are all seeing up to 10,000 ads a day.* Any time you're trying to snag your customer's attention, that's what you're competing with. If you're selling shoes, you're not just competing against other shoe companies for your customer's attention. You're competing against baby-food companies, book-sellers, bicycle manufacturers, and every other type of company you can imagine. Everyone is competing for the same limited amount of attention.

Many business owners see marketing as a straightforward way to get people into their sales pipeline.

Wrong. Marketing is a bloodbath—and if you don't see it that way, you'll be dead soon.

How does your company stand out in that sea of information? How do you make sure you're undefeated in the battle for people's attention and money?

Do you think a clunky website is going to cut it? Do you think a generic video is going to win someone over? Do you think high-lighting your company's brand—without ever giving a thought to what your customers or clients really want or desire—is going to cut through the noise?

No way.

You must get into the customer data game!

Most marketers will tell you, "We have lots of data." What they mean is that they use Google and Facebook Analytics. (This costs them nothing, meaning they're acting like they're helping you when, really, they're trying to cut corners.) Don't get me wrong. Those can be helpful, but there are better options out there. Even marketers know it! According to Crowd Research Partners, 42%

of marketers think that the lack of quality data is their largest obstacle when it comes to implementing successful campaigns. That's a staggering number.

Of course, they don't tell their clients that. They brag about their Google Analytics and pretend like it's great, because who's going to tell a client, "We aren't generating as many leads as we could because our data sucks"? Those types of marketers are out of a job fast.

In those marketers' minds, they're doing the best they can because that's how everyone else does it too. When it comes to data, they're following the status quo. But let me tell you, the status quo is behind the times. When you're competing against 9,999 other ads for a person's attention, the status quo isn't going to cut it. You have to think differently with your marketing. And I assume that's why you're here, reading this book. I will show you how to break through the noise as we move through each chapter.

We are living in the most disruptive time in human history, and 25% to 30% of all malls are predicted to close in the next few years. Fox Business recently reported on the pending "Apocalypse" of the brick-and-mortar retail economy. E-commerce has been the driver of this Armageddon, but after COVID-19 and the looming advancement of virtual reality and augmented reality, you can expect there to be a knockout punch soon. And it should scare the hell out of anyone in this space.

My friend, serial entrepreneur Peter Diamandis, recently wrote, "Already, several big players have broken into the VR market... Walmart filed 2 VR shopping-related patents. In a new bid to disrupt a rapidly changing retail market, Walmart now describes a system in which users couple their VR headset with haptic gloves for an immersive in-store experience, whether at 3 a.m., in your living room, or during a lunch break at the office."

While the 2020 pandemic and VR/AR disruption are happening more rapidly in this industry than others, I also see a gap that might save some of those retailers and your business as well.

Disruptive technology is not building a deeper connection with the customer yet. It's only based on convenience.

Convenience? Absolutely. But not a human connection. And therein lies an opportunity for you.

So, if you want your business to grow even more, you need to think differently. You need to have better customer/client data because *that's* what's going to help you stand out. Those that invest in a deeper understanding of their customers will flourish. Those that don't will die.

I don't say that to scare you. I say it because you have to know what you're up against. Status quo, data-starved marketing isn't going to stand up to the disruption I am seeing, and I believe at least 95% of our economy will be disrupted in the next 5 to 10 years.

Time is running out for you. Are you going to sit idly by?

If you're overwhelmed by the amount of disruption, or if you're not sure how to take your head out of the sand and move forward, here's my advice: start easy in understanding your customers. Do your research on them, ask them questions (either 1-on-1 or through surveys), and listen to what they really want. Then, when you are ready to take the next step, dig even deeper and invest in a more sophisticated approach until you have a crystal-clear understanding of what your customer data says. The bottom line to breaking through with your marketing is that you must deeply understand your customers before you can empathetically appeal to them.

That's the very first step to making a powerful, innovative change. Get some initial wins on the board, and it will change your mindset and thrust you forward.

HOW UNDERSTANDING YOUR CUSTOMER DATA CONVERTS MORE SALES

New Hampshire's incumbent Republican governor, Chris Sununu, was looking down the barrel of a gun.

Three months before the election, it seemed like it was going to be a blue wave cycle, meaning polling predicted that Democrats were going to sweep elected offices around the country. Sununu couldn't just rest on his laurels and expect to come out on top. His campaign knew victory was going to take some initiative and ingenuity.

From a political perspective, there are a few things you need to know about New Hampshire. First, it tends to lean blue. That's already a hard pill for a Republican governor to swallow, but it's especially daunting in the face of a blue wave.

Second, it's more common for women to hold political positions in New Hampshire than in most other states. That doesn't mean that women are more likely to win. But it did mean that Sununu's female Democratic opponent wasn't fighting an uphill battle because of her gender.

Third, although the state leans Democratic these days, there's a streak of libertarianism that runs deep in the state as well. Taxation is *always* a contentious issue. "Broad-based taxes" might as well be a curse word for a lot of New Hampshirites. This third point was the Sununu campaign's bread and butter. That's why they had run a whole series of TV and digital ads boasting about New Hampshire's economic successes.

Imagine how flabbergasted Sununu's campaign was when they learned he was down in the polls and those ads weren't cutting it. *Why weren't the usual talking points working?* It was up to us to find a way to fight off that looming blue wave.

With only 3 months to go, we had to work quickly, but we also knew we couldn't cut corners. That's what political marketing is all about—working on a tight timeline *while getting it right*. In politics, there are no do-overs. There's no room for sloppy mistakes, and there are no ties. There is only win or lose.

Instead of relying on what we already thought we knew about voters, we went back to square one. We took a deep dive into the New Hampshire voter data to learn who our key base of voters really was and what kind of issues they cared about most.

What we found blew us away.

The Sununu campaign had been off to a good start. Early in the race, one of their main strategies was to siphon support away from their female opponent by focusing on winning over independent women voters. Our data showed that strategy was spot-on.

The problem was that women voters weren't responding to the campaign's messaging. So, if ads about economic success weren't doing the trick, what were they getting wrong? What was going to convince these independent women voters to reelect Sununu?

Isn't this the same question business owners ask themselves every day? How can I convince my customers to show up? How can I create such passion in my customers that they keep coming back, time and time again?

Here's the bottom line. When you want to know what's going to motivate your customers and clients, always go back to your data to understand what motivates them to take action. There's a story buried in that research, and that story has everything you need. It holds the key to the vital question *What do my customers and clients really want?*

When we dove deeper into the voter data about these independent women voters, we found our answer. The Sununu camp had focused their attention on ads celebrating low unemployment rates and tax cuts, but women didn't give a damn about that. They were half as likely as men to watch those kinds of ads.

So, what did they care about?

Well, they *did* care about the economy. The Sununu camp had gotten that right.

But it wasn't enough for independent women voters to know that Sununu had implemented tax cuts and reforms. They wanted to know how those tax cuts and reforms affected their families.

Did the reforms create higher-paying jobs? Did the tax cuts take money away from their children's schools? Our data (Step 1) clearly showed the distinction—where men cared about the policy, women cared about the *impact*.

Once we knew those distinctions, it was easy to design a marketing strategy (Step 2) that spoke specifically to those swing independent women voters that we targeted on digital media. We ran a new ad tailored for those female voters that drove home how Governor Sununu had been a champion for families. Who doesn't love the idea of full-day kindergarten, child protection reform, and safer schools? We left independent women voters with one key statement ringing in their ears: "As a mom, I'm thankful for Chris Sununu."

More than 70% of our target group of independent women voters who saw the ad watched it all the way through to the end, which is a pretty good indicator that it worked. Just think, would you watch a political ad on the internet all the way to the end unless it resonated with you? No. You'd probably click the "Skip ad" button. The new messaging was hitting its mark.

In the end, Governor Sununu closed out the race strong, and he won reelection. It's safe to say that if the Sununu campaign hadn't regrouped, that race could have been lost.

Because we took such a long, hard look at what the data was telling us about New Hampshire voters, we knew exactly whom to target (independent women) and how (a family-oriented economic angle) to create messaging that would take hold.

Converting voters isn't all that different from converting customers or clients. If you want them to search for you, visit your website, or click "buy," you have to tap into what they're about and what motivates them to buy. You have to give them a reason to build a relationship with you.

I've met so many business owners who make the same mistake. When I ask, "What does your customer want?" their reply is wishy-washy or vague. They tell me things like "We want to reach millennials" or "Moms are our key demographic."

No. That's who your ideal customers are. That has nothing to do with what they want.

The only way you can get to the bottom of what customers want is by using consumer data and analytics to understand not just who your customer is, but what, deep down, motivates them. Customer data is your key to empathy.

It's not enough to know that your ideal customer is 35, female, and sporty. You have to know what drives her. What desire or value gets her out of bed in the morning? Is she sporty because she wants to be healthy? Because she wants to look good? Because she's an adrenaline junkie who lives for adventure? Because she's competitive and wants to beat all her friends at CrossFit?

That may sound like an exaggeration, but trust me. It isn't. That's how deep you have to go if you want to really get to know your customer, eliminate your marketing risk, and ensure your dollars are always ROI-positive. *That's* what you have to tap into.

I've worked with so many business owners who think they know what their customers want, when really, they're just guessing. When it comes to your clients or customers, are you making assumptions or are you tuned into their wants, desires, and needs?

You can't build a business on guesses. Comprehensive, systematic customer/client data is the most powerful tool you have to create marketing that resonates with your audience.

If you're out there swimming in a sea of 10,000 ads, and your only life preserver is a bunch of guesses, your chances of survival aren't great. That's a lesson a lot of businesses learn the hard way—especially in times of disruption.

THE COMING DISRUPTION WILL HIT YOUR BUSINESS HARD

When it comes to your business, things are always changing. But sometimes the pace is slower than others.

I'm always looking at consumer data on a daily basis. I eat, sleep, and breathe a steady flow of preferences, trends, and patterns. For 12 years after the 2008 Great Recession, consumer data consistently pointed us toward 4 messaging themes with constant traction: image, excitement, pleasure, and luxury.

For example, during those 10 years, Coca-Cola was running ads featuring people in bathing suits on a beach, drinking a Coke, living it up, and having fun. Social media platform ads showed people with opulent lives with novelty at every turn. Yachts, epic vistas, luxury vacations, parties filled with beautiful people and decadent booze. People wanted picture-perfect scenery, picture-perfect apparel—basically, picture-perfect everything.

Simply put, consumers wanted other people to look at them, with their higher status, and feel envy.

It might sound crass, but you know what I'm talking about. You've seen the images with some 20-something Instagram influencer giving the camera a stare so intense you can almost read their mind: *Hey, look at me. I'm on a beach. I've got half my clothes on, and I'm wearing a watch you should buy.* There were influencers who were doing nothing but traveling the world, looking glamorous, and getting paid big bucks. And it worked. People bought it.

And this whole envy-inducing party was built on the shoulders of social media. When social media first hit the scene, it began as a movement—quite literally. Social media started by helping political movements around the world take shape. Pretty quickly, though, it became a "biz" with a pay-to-play model, and within 10 years, it was a full-fledged racket where everything was focused on status and envy.

Before the coronavirus pandemic hit in 2020, we were living in what I like to call an "Instagram influencer economy." And it was thriving. Big followings led to big money. For example, the BBC reported that in 2019, advertisers paid Kylie Jenner $1.2 million per Instagram post, in the hopes that her 141 million followers would see their products and follow Kylie's lead.

That's the extreme, but it filtered down to communities all over America, where local "influencers" were getting paid well to advertise local brands.

Marketers weren't just touting the glamorous, luxury lifestyle for no reason. Consumers were hungry for anything that smacked of splendor. *They craved it.*

The consumer data I looked at during this time period revealed that looking successful and smart; acquiring wealth, status, and influence; and having a life full of excitement were at the top of consumers' buying priorities.

And when I say "the top," I mean *the top*. Looking good, being wealthy, and leading an exciting life took precedence over everything, including convenience, security, family, safety—you name it.

That's why Uber, a business that could position itself entirely around convenience, ran ads showing a tuxedoed person using their black car service. The tagline? "When black tie isn't really optional."

Now, you and I both know that day-to-day, most Uber users weren't flitting off to glamorous parties. But that's the image the company portrayed *because that's what customers wanted to be.*

Companies knew it. Marketers knew it. The whole world knew

it. If you were in any area of advertising, "aspirational" was the name of the game. Whether you were Uber, Coca-Cola, or Nike, you were running ads that touted pleasure.

Maybe Coca-Cola put it best: "Open a Coke, open happiness."

Then COVID-19 hit. Between late February and the first week of April, the stock market tanked. Americans were put on lockdown, travel halted, and some industries disappeared overnight.

Talk about disruption.

In a matter of weeks, Americans completely reprioritized their life values and—for the first time in 10 years—their spending habits. With everyone stuck at home during lockdown, no one wanted to see people flaunting their "happiness" (or wealth or high social status).

The big companies figured that out immediately.

How? They are constantly on top of the latest consumer data trends because they invest big dollars in it. They know every time their customer base breathes, much less stops spending. That's how they built billion-dollar companies. And if you want your business to grow in these unprecedented, disruptive times, that's what you have to do too—even if you have a small marketing budget.

Uber quickly pivoted their message away from black cars and stressed, "A company that moves people is asking you not to move. Together we can stop this." Coca-Cola quickly switched gears and announced, "Staying apart is the best way to stay united."

They read the writing on the wall and knew that tuxedos weren't going to cut it in the middle of a global pandemic.

Unfortunately, some people didn't seem to get the memo. When the lockdown orders came, a California business owner I knew laid off a bunch of employees. The next weekend, he and his wife went out on their luxury boat. My friend's wife posted a photo on social media. She was wearing a bikini and proudly holding up a glass of wine. The caption read, "Living My Best Coronalife."

Come on.

People who had been laid off from their company followed her on social media, and she got eviscerated. Rightfully so. It was painfully tone-deaf. People were suffering. They were locked down, out of work, and had loved ones who were sick or dying. Nobody wanted to know how good she looked, how much fun she was having, or how she was living her best "coronalife."

It didn't matter that bikini-clad influencers had been posting that stuff just a month earlier and making millions of dollars off of it. Overnight, the messaging that had worked for nearly a decade took a nosedive.

It was a great lesson to learn. *You cannot be tone-deaf to your customers.* If you are, not only will you not grow your business, but you might even be destroyed.

Now, you might say my friend's wife should have known better. It's just basic common sense to not flaunt your good fortune in the middle of a global pandemic and economic meltdown.

But, on another level, think about it from a business owner's perspective. When you've been doing something for 10 years, and suddenly it doesn't work anymore, that's a gut punch. If you don't know how to quickly pivot, the wind will get knocked out of you.

Imagine that disruption is a bull, he's mad as hell, and you're alone in the ring with him. He's going to come for you, one way or another. There's no escape.

Would you rather face that bull head-on or turn your back and look the other way?

The answer seems like a no-brainer. But let me tell you, I have seen so many business owners get gored in the back because they "assumed" they already had all the answers. They thought their marketing team had their fingers on the pulse of the zeitgeist. But when push came to shove, they only had tired tactics, false assumptions, and outdated ideas about their customers. In other words, these business owners had a death wish and didn't know it.

When you don't know what your customers want or desire—when you haven't learned to empathize with them on a *deep* level—you're playing with fire.

Sure, the coronavirus situation was unique. In 24 years of marketing, I've never seen the marketing world shift that dramatically. But consumer preferences are *always* changing, and the next big disruptor is always on the horizon. You and your business should always be ready to stare the bull in the face—and take it by the horns.

COVID-19 left so many unprepared businesses and brands in its wake. During that initial moment of lockdowns, if you were an "influencer" without any real substance to your brand, you were dead. If you were a business consultant or coach without any valid credentials, you were in deep trouble. If you had a business that exploited status and significance, you had to pivot that message immediately.

How did we know that? The data told us so in real time.

In January 2020, we surveyed 4,888 American consumers on their purchasing behaviors. We modeled the results to our database of more than 200 million American profiles, which are based on billions of up-to-the-moment trackable consumer purchasing decisions. So we had an incredibly sophisticated understanding of what motivated these consumers' choices.

Then the pandemic hit, and we knew we had to get a grasp on what was going on with consumers—and we had to do it fast. Right after most stay-at-home orders went into effect, we resurveyed the same group of 4,888 people. Because we were able to compare the results between consumers right *before* and right *after* the pandemic hit, we knew exactly how their perspectives and behaviors had changed.

In other words, we had the most sophisticated data study *in the world* in our hands when no business owner had a clue what was going to happen next.

Here's what we found. When we asked respondents which personal values influenced their decisions the most, the majority of consumers said "helping and caring for family and friends," "preserving your own safety and the safety of your family," and "being dependable and trustworthy for family and friends." When we asked them which personal values affected their daily decisions, including personal actions and products they buy, the same 3 values rose to the top.

In essence, the top 3 messages consumers wanted to hear from any business marketing to them in March of 2020 were how their product or service helped others, created safety, and cultivated trust.

And what do you think the lowest-ranking values were?

You guessed it: being in charge and directing people, being successful and admired for your achievements, and acquiring wealth, status, and influence.

Hello, Instagram influencer economy! Your days were numbered!

No one wanted the tried-and-true influencer messaging. They wanted messaging that assured safety and security for their loved ones and themselves. They wanted to feel "We're all in this together" not "Look at me—I stand apart." They needed reassurance, familiarity, and comfort. Novelty went out the window.

To put it bluntly, consumers made a 180-degree pivot. They were no longer buying things they *wanted*. They were only buying things they *needed*. When families were looking to cut their family budgets, they were asking themselves, "Do I want this, or do I need this?"

That was great news for businesses like our national pest control client. We helped them go all-in on their pandemic marketing because we knew that with people quarantined and cooking every meal at home during springtime, there was going to be an influx of bugs and pests that could carry disease. But we knew, with families cutting budgets, we had to frame these services as a "need."

We shifted our messaging to hit those core themes of trust, safety, and helping others. We stressed, "During a pandemic, you don't want potential disease carriers in your family's home. We'll come in to help your family stay safe. We'll wear face coverings and gloves, and stay socially distanced. You can also trust us to keep your dog safe while you're out of the house." Bottom line, we gave them reassurance.

But a lot of other businesses didn't realize they had to shift their messaging. They were chugging along with their campaigns as usual—*because they weren't tracking their consumers' shifting preferences*. They had no idea what their customers wanted.

Surprise, surprise. Over a matter of months, the Instagram influencer economy bombed. According to Fox Business, 2020 was the first time that there had ever been a drop in fees for influencers, including the highest earners. Kylie Jenner even lost her billionaire status.

It took marketing teams a while to figure out that people didn't want to see the lives of the rich and famous when they were stuck in a 2-bedroom apartment with a toddler all day. Business owners stopped paying influencers.

But let me be clear. When it comes to marketing, hope won't get you too far. That was a lesson too many companies learned the hard way, and by the time they realized the ship was sinking, it was already too late for some of them.

During that wild, disruptive moment, many companies were operating in fear. They were trying to conserve money, and one of the first things they cut was their marketing budget.

Meanwhile, companies that *did* follow consumer purchasing data knew how their customers were responding to the pandemic, and they knew what messages would work to increase their ROI during that massively disruptive economic moment. They shifted their messaging, and they shifted it fast.

Know what else? They also realized they were being given a massive opportunity. If they managed to navigate that crazy, uncertain moment, they could easily distinguish themselves from the competition and make huge gains while their competitors sat on their hands.

These savvy companies knew this was exactly the moment when they should be putting themselves out there. They seized the opportunity to invest even more of their ad dollars and push themselves ahead of their competitors.

Companies like Instacart and Postmates enacted policies that allowed deliveries to be left at people's doors. Then they promoted those services as the best way to limit personal interaction. Customers immediately knew that those companies were there to *help* and *trusted* that these companies would *safely* deliver creature comforts to their homes. Bingo! They nailed the trifecta for pandemic success.

Here's another example. One of our clients was a furniture company with stores throughout the Southeast, and we ran ads for them with the core message "We've been in the community for 104 years. We're your local furniture store. We've helped families during this horrible COVID-19 moment. Where were the big, national furniture chains in your community? What have they been doing during this time?" That message crushed it for them. (It was also a comparatising ad, which you will learn about more in Chapter 8.)

Here's the lesson for you. When disruption hits hard, don't shy away. Figure out how your customers are changing their purchasing habits. Then commit to changing with them.

HOW DO I LOOK AT CONSUMER DATA?

I have a partnership with the largest data analytics and AI company in America, which means that we have access to unfathomable amounts of consumer data. But what exactly is this data, and how does it work? What goes into our proprietary Customer Insights Report?

Broadly speaking, there are 3 kinds of consumer data that will help you get a clear idea about what motivates your customer. The first is consumer research databases. These reveal how and why people make the buying decisions they do. Let's say you own an e-commerce retail store, and you've noticed that a lot of customers are adding merchandise to their carts but stop before completing the checkout. No one likes to see that kind of money left on the table.

For example, your customers may gravitate toward websites

with free shipping. When they realize they'll have to pay an extra $15.99 to FedEx the item to themselves, they abandon their cart. Consumer research databases might help you figure out what's keeping them from pulling the "buy" trigger.

The second kind of data focuses on online behavioral and contextual research. How are people using their devices? What keywords are they searching for, and how do they operate online? Do they use Instagram more than LinkedIn, or do they rely on social media or e-commerce platforms to make purchases?

Remember my hair care client who found out that Pinterest was going to be their *real* moneymaker and that Facebook was going to be next to useless? Online behavioral research tells you everything you need to know about your customers' behaviors and habits.

Thirdly, demographic data can tell you a lot about the life experiences and values of your customers. Don't just look at age and gender. Consider aspects like household income, education, and marital status. Are most of your customers in their twenties, living with roommates, and working their way through college? If so, messaging about providing for their families probably won't be as effective as content focused on saving money and time. If, on the other hand, your customers are primarily middle-aged suburban parents with multiple children and steady, white-collar jobs, an advertisement with a bunch of pretty young things at a party probably won't resonate.

This may sound obvious, but you'd be surprised at how often marketers employ a "one-size-fits-all" marketing strategy for their clients. They get so caught up in creating content, branding, and selling *your business* that they forget that marketing isn't really about your business at all. Marketing is about tapping into what makes your customers tick.

When you put all 3 groups of information together, you'll have enough for a Customer Insights Report, which helps gauge exactly who your target customer is and what will motivate them to buy from you.

Here's how the Customer Insights Report worked for one of our clients during the pandemic. This client—an organic product company that sells items like toothpaste, soap, and cosmetics—didn't only want to lean into the coronavirus messaging pivot. They wanted to *dominate* their market space, so they actually committed even more of their financial resources during the crisis. They saw an opportunity where others only saw shark-infested waters. I love these kinds of outlier business owners.

Our goal was to reposition their marketing so their entire messaging focused on the 3 magic coronavirus values: safety, trust, and helping others.

Our data showed that out of 200 million American consumers, 150 million were actively searching for coronavirus-related products. So, right off the bat, we knew we could eliminate 50 million people from our target audience because they weren't engaged.

Then, out of the 150 million, we were able to segment out vegans and vegetarians, who were much more likely to buy organic products. Almost immediately, we had much more precise targets to build our strategic campaign around. We knew who our "bull's-eye" customers were going to be.

Next, we decided which geographic regions had the lowest-hanging fruit—that way, our client would earn an almost immediate ROI. If you were like most business owners—whose marketing teams let assumptions lead the way—here's where you may have gotten things dead wrong.

You might assume it would be a bad idea to market organic products in coronavirus hot spots. After all, many people in those areas were in a financial crunch and were conserving their cash. They might look at organic products, which are more expensive, and think, *I want fancy organic soap, but I don't really need it. It's a frivolous expense.*

Wrong.

Instead, our research showed that sales in New York, which was a hot spot at the time, far outperformed other markets, as customers were actively searching online for products that would keep them healthy. We just had to make sure that New Yorkers saw the products as necessities. They had to feel like chemical-free organic soap was going to improve their immune system and help them stay healthy and comfortable in that scary moment.

Based on our data, we developed a strategy around COVID-friendly messaging. We rebranded their message, and when we tested our messages, the line that worked best was "Don't compromise on your family's health with toxic products." Another line that performed well was "Horrified by the ingredients in your skincare products?" The third message that worked focused explicitly on safety: "We make safe, natural, plant-powered products that support your immunity."

When our client launched those ads, they were the highest-performing ads they'd ever had. All because our client invested in a deep understanding of the consumer market and followed through on what the data told us would matter most to their customers.

DON'T REFUSE THE MAP

In 2016, Donald Trump mostly crushed his Republican presidential opponents across the country, but during the Iowa caucuses, Ted Cruz came out ahead.

Why? What set Cruz apart in such a tight race?

Simple. He had a clear understanding of what Republican primary-voting Iowans cared about. He branded himself differently. He showed them that in a sea of Republican candidates, he was the one who was relevant and unique. He was the one aligned with their values.

That's a great lesson for your business too. *If you want your business to flourish, you must be both relevant and unique to the customer—from their perspective, not yours.*

When business was booming for "social media influencers," they didn't have any reason to try to understand their followers/customers better. It was all about "me."

What they didn't realize was that they weren't successful because of *who they were*. They were successful because customers *valued the things they represented*: status, power, and luxury. Once those values shifted, the influencers who weren't able to match new value systems got left behind.

Is your marketing founded on a deep understanding of what your customers and clients think, feel, and want? Or are you just throwing something up on a website—which I call "spraying and praying"?

In today's world, status quo marketing isn't just "okay." It's downright risky. It's time to follow the 5-step formula and make data the core of your marketing campaign.

Understanding your customer or ideal target market is critical, and consumer data is your map. It helps you find your way and make sure your business is always on track. We all know that maps are useful, but according to marketing legend Seth Godin, "Sometimes, when we're lost, we refuse a map, even when offered. Because the map reminds us that we made a mistake. That we were wrong."

As a general rule in life, most people refuse change until the pain is too great. Just look at how I handled my own health a decade ago. I didn't shift until the pain was too great. Many business owners don't proactively seek better marketing until they've already suffered losses. They trust their marketing agency blindly and find themselves in a mess. Maybe their business is failing, or maybe their sales have stalled and now their competitors are crushing them because they've wasted precious dollars on failed ad campaigns.

Don't refuse the map. Without it, you're not only wrong; you will remain lost. It's not worth it to stick with a behind-the-times, inadequate approach to understanding your customers and clients, even if it seems to be working in the short run.

Take the map and take action now. Once you're lost, it's much harder to get out of the forest. Look at what the map tells you, come up with a strategy, and chart your course *before* shit hits the fan.

So how do you take the first right step to implement the Undefeated Marketing System? Regarding data (Step 1), yes, I have a very committed and sophisticated platform, but there are hundreds of other consumer data companies out there that take similar approaches. Some are really expensive, while others are affordable. Do some research and commit to a data-backed approach before you spend another dollar on marketing.

CHAPTER 3

STEP 2: BUILD YOUR DATA-BACKED STRATEGIC MARKETING PLAN

IN A RECENT US CONGRESSIONAL RACE, THE DEMOCRATIC Congressional Campaign Committee had set its sights on winning a hotly contested election in Central Texas. It was one of their biggest targets across the whole country.

The Republican incumbent was Congressman Roger Williams, and he knew that he was facing the toughest election of his career. Democrats all across the country were pouring money into the campaign of his challenger, Julie Oliver. The COVID pandemic had caused a massive, unanticipated disruption, and a wave of anti-Trump sentiment was sweeping segments of the country.

For the first time in decades, it looked like Democrats might have a chance of turning Texas blue, and all eyes were on Roger's district. It included a large part of Democrat-leaning Austin,

Texas, and in the previous election, 2 years earlier, Roger had only received 34% of the vote there.

In other words, this was going to be a *tight* race.

Roger reached out to us in April, near the beginning of the pandemic, to create a comprehensive marketing campaign that would lead him to victory. We immediately took a deep dive into the voter data to see what his constituents cared about and what would motivate them to take action (Step 1).

Here's what we found. Due to all the uncertainty people were experiencing because of COVID-19, they really wanted a political candidate who cared about their lives, their health, and their livelihood, and who was willing to listen to their concerns. They were also worried about healthcare, and more specifically, in light of the pandemic, they were afraid that insurance protections for preexisting conditions might be taken away. All in all, our data research told us these target voters craved a sense of safety and security.

Next, we built a strategic marketing plan around our voter data (Step 2), and we realized that the pandemic had given us a unique marketing opportunity. In April 2020, no one was spending money on ads, due to the massive amount of uncertainty in the world, so advertising was cheap. Meanwhile, people were staying home and spending a lot more time online. That was the perfect double-whammy for a successful online campaign. There was no competition for getting our message out, and because no one else was running ads, we had the opportunity to control the narrative.

Our strategic plan included kicking off the campaign well before our opponent with an online survey that would allow us to get an even deeper understanding of voter sentiment and collect interested voters' contact information. This gave us the chance to communicate 1-on-1 with engaged voters, and it showed these voters that Roger was deeply invested in connecting with them during that turbulent time. He was the candidate prepared to give them the care, consideration, and safety our Step 1 data had told us they desperately wanted.

We knew from our data dive that our strategic plan needed an extensive peer-to-peer texting campaign, which would help build even deeper relationships with our target voters. Instead of getting the same generic text sent to thousands of other voters, our target voters received individual communication based on their concerns from the survey they took, which made them feel special and cared for. When it comes to building a connection with voters, customers, or clients, a personal touch is always 1,000 times more effective than bland bulk communication.

Next, we built Roger's brand (Step 3) around that data-backed strategic plan. Our online survey was topped with the caption "I'm listening. What issues matter to you right now?" Beneath it, prospective voters saw a picture of Roger, wearing a kind smile in front of a gentle yet optimistic yellow background. In an instant, our branding (based on the voter data insights) showed voters that Roger wasn't a candidate trying to blindly push an agenda. He was a candidate who sincerely cared about what his constituents had to say.

Because we already knew that voters were worried about healthcare and we knew that Democrats were going to attack Roger on the question of preexisting conditions, we also filmed a video ad to allay voters' fears. Roger spoke directly to the camera about his own preexisting condition as a cancer survivor, which helped build a deeply personal and emotional connection with viewers.

We followed the data (Step 1). We mapped out our strategic plan (Step 2). We branded our campaign around this data (Step 3). We tested our ads (Step 4), and then we launched (Step 5) well ahead of our opponent.

By the time Julie Oliver's campaign ran an attack ad on this issue months later, we were already one step ahead. We had already established with voters that Roger wasn't a threat to their healthcare needs. Better yet, we showed them that his firsthand experience with a preexisting condition gave him unique insight into what voters needed. What would you trust more? A late-in-the-game attack ad, or an up-front, candid heart-to-heart conversation with a cancer survivor?

On Election Day, not only did Roger Williams win a tough race, but he had *the largest margin of victory* (14 points) out of the races targeted by the Democratic Congressional Campaign Committee.

Now, remember that this was supposed to be one of the tightest races in the country. Do you know why it wasn't?

Because we had an aggressive and better strategy that we *knew* was going to work because we followed the 5-step Undefeated Marketing System. That kind of success doesn't happen by luck. It was the result of solid research and data on the voters, and we built a comprehensive strategy for what was going to drive Roger's supporters to action.

Your business can experience the same kind of success. You just have to follow the steps. Once you've developed a clear understanding of your customers or clients, you must implement Step 2 and build a marketing strategy that effectively speaks to your customers or clients.

BUILD YOUR STRATEGY AROUND YOUR OUTCOMES AND YOUR CUSTOMERS' VALUES AND MOTIVATIONS

One of my corporate marketing clients is a dream for anyone who likes superhero movies or sci-fi. Seriously. They came up with a product that feels like it's straight out of a futuristic blockbuster, and the demonstration videos are enough to blow your mind. More importantly, the product also has the potential to solve a huge societal problem and save millions of lives.

Think of this product as "remote handcuffs." It's a device that looks like a Taser but allows users to safely and humanely apprehend a criminal suspect by shooting a Kevlar rope from up to 25 feet away. The rope shoots out at a rate of 513 feet per second and wraps itself around the suspect before they have time to think. It's called the BolaWrap.

This tool is the perfect low-force alternative to other devices on a cop's duty belt, like batons, pepper spray, and Tasers. It was created so law enforcement and the military can de-escalate tense situations while apprehending suspects. It also decreases the potential that any bystanders, officers, or suspects will get hurt.

In the age of Black Lives Matter and counter Blue Lives Matter movements, this product was uniquely situated to make multiple demographics happy. Not only does it protect law enforcement officers and prevent crime, but it also minimizes harm to suspects. That's a win-win for 2 demographics who rarely see eye to eye.

There was just 1 problem. This client's product and brand were relatively unknown, and their stock price was undervalued—hovering in the mid-single digits since its initial public offering. The challenge for investors in this company was clear: *How do we tell our story, increase our stock valuation to outside investors, and leverage it to create widespread investor momentum for the company?*

To figure out what would resonate with new backers, we created a comprehensive Investor Insights Report that matched 190,000 target investors with millions of data points, consisting of consumer interests, psychological drivers, and daily habits. Our data showed that potential investors fit the following criteria:

- Annual stock investment between $50,000 and $3 million
- A college-level education or higher
- Male, over 35 years of age
- Based in the northeast United States

We also uncovered several key personal and psychological values that mattered to this group of potential backers. For example, they cared about social significance and looking important to their peers, and they had a high interest in tolerance and acceptance of others. Their hobbies or interests included a passion for politics, specifically supporting issues surrounding African Americans, gun control, and de-escalating the use of police force.

This painted a pretty clear picture of our target investor market. In layman's terms, you could call them "limousine liberals." They lean toward liberal political values, like gun control and social justice, but they aren't blue-collar union workers. They're rich and have some degree of influence and power.

Our data told us these people frequently give to charity—not because of some burning passion to help others—but mostly because of the status it confers among their peer group. Social position was a powerful motivator for this group.

To be clear, I don't mean any of that as a criticism. (A dollar given to charity is another dollar that charity didn't have, and I'm all for any kind of philanthropy.) The reason I raise the "status" element here is because it cuts to the core of our strategy. If you don't understand your audience's core motivations, you won't be able to effectively reach them. And that's what the data told us our target investors' motivations were.

Once we had a clear, data-driven understanding of our target investor market (Step 1), our next step was creating a solid strategy that would make them take action (Step 2).

If I were to give you the "bumper sticker" definition of a data-backed strategic marketing plan, here it is. You must marry your company's desired outcome with your target customer's needs. The goal you want *must* be in alignment with your customer's values, which is why Step 1 is so important. You can't come up with a strategy that works if you have no idea what your customer wants, values, and needs.

Your strategy should take the following elements into consideration:

- What platforms your audience uses
- What language appeals to your audience
- Which values your clients and customers care most about
- What media platform your customers spend the most time consuming, and what will most effectively move them to conversion
- Your timeline to accomplish your outcomes
- Your budget to spend and the corresponding ROI multiple

In a nutshell, your strategy is your 1-stop-shop game plan or North Star that will pave the way for every ounce of branding and content you create (Step 3), message testing you employ (Step 4), and advertising you launch (Step 5). This is where you sit down and distill all the information you collected in Step 1 into an actionable step-by-step plan.

It's kind of like this: when you own a business, you must have a 5- to 10-year business plan. You don't just play it by ear every day. You create a game plan around your vision. The same thing applies to your marketing.

For our Marvel Universe–esque client, we needed to figure out *exactly* how we were going to reach these target limousine liberal investors to become investors in the company. What language would speak to their love of "status"? Where did they hang out online? What was the creative medium that would move their needle? We took the time to lay out *every aspect of our plan* before we ever started creating ads or pushing content in their general direction.

You can think of marketing like hunting deer. Who do you think the more successful hunter is going to be? The guy who walks into the woods, sits down, and says, "Well, I hope something walks by me so I can shoot it" or the person who spends months finding deer tracks, understanding deer trails, and learning how the deer move and where they bed down at night so, when hunting season begins, they know exactly where to go because they know the behavioral patterns of the deer?

If you want to be in the marketing game, you need a clear strategy. Otherwise, you're just wasting time and money.

For this particular client, our data showed that a highly emotional and engaging video was going to be the best way to reach our potential target investors, so we planned to create a 30-second spot. Then, also based on what we knew from the data (seeing a theme here?), we determined what type of messaging would encourage these investors to take action. The final piece of our strategic plan used our data (surprise, surprise) to determine which social media platforms would align with our client's budget and needs. We planned a 24-day, 5-figure ad campaign delivered to 190,000 potential investors.

By the time we moved to creating content (Step 3), our strategy had already identified 4 key elements that would make our video successful. (You can find the video at winbigmedia.com.)

- **Grab immediate attention.** Short attention spans require immediate intrigue, so our video began with the product being fired into the air. It's a stunning piece of technology on its own, but seeing that 8-foot rope soar through the air at lightning speed is like magic.
- **Increase credibility and validation.** Once we grabbed the target audience's attention, we had to keep it. We couldn't just yell, "This is the best product ever!" We had to show high-status third-party validations that showed the company's legitimacy. Because the target audience placed a high value on "status," we paraded every high-profile news source we could. We gave them a glimpse of an interview with the company's CEO on Fox Business's highest-rated show. We showed the Fox Business anchor brandishing the Taser-like tool with wide-eyed excitement. We hit them hard and fast with prominent mainstream media outlets that had featured the product as well: Bloomberg News, NBC, ABC, CBS. There was no way they could walk away with doubts about the product's credibility.
- **Increase curiosity.** If you want somebody to watch a video, you have to create curiosity, so our next move was to amplify the intrigue we had already developed. We underscored the "significance" of the product using phrases like "revolutionary" and "the next great company." We also included clips from the device's use in the hit TV show *NCIS: Los Angeles*. This portion of the video would increase intrigue among investors, giving them the idea that they could be buying into a game-changing stock at a bottom-floor price. This tactic spoke to the value they placed on status, significance, and respect.
- **Educate and create urgency.** The last 10 seconds of the

video were designed to elicit action. We featured content from CBS News's *Sunday Morning* that demonstrated the use of the innovative product, which further underscored its significance. Then we ended with a line from the segment: "This could change the way police do their jobs," followed by the company's stock symbol.

Our creative content (Step 3) drilled down on the messaging that we knew would motivate potential investors. But—and this is important—*we couldn't have gotten to that perfect Step 3 without gathering the target investor data in Step 1 and developing a clear strategy in Step 2.*

Take a look back at those 4 key video elements. Every single one of them speaks to the psychological drivers and values held by our target investors. Every single one of them is part of a clear plan, designed to speak directly to our 190,000-person target audience. Nothing about the video was left to chance.

We tested our messaging just to make sure it was resonating in all the right ways with all the right people (Step 4—and it did), and by the time we launched the campaign (Step 5), we knew that our strategy would work.

What were the results? Our video had an engagement rate *double* the national average. The ad was watched to completion 541,654 times, even though we directly targeted only 190,000 potential investors. That means twice as many target investors clicked through the video to visit the company's investor page, and it was viewed multiple times to completion by our target investor audience.

If those numbers sound abstract, let me put it this way: our video was a resounding success because it spoke directly to our audience's values. It was something that got their attention and built intrigue, so they watched it all the way through on digital platforms and social media.

And even though we'll get to it more in Step 3, here's something I want to stress: you *must* have creative content that speaks to your customers' emotions. You might follow the 5 steps to a T, but if you develop boring, unemotional creative content, you won't get results. The whole point of using a data-backed strategy is to make your customer *feel* something. Whether that's self-importance, laughter, excitement, or any variety of emotions—that will depend on who your customer is. But no matter what, *make them feel*. Otherwise, all the strategy in the world will be useless.

Target investors watched our client's video because it was exciting, curious, powerful. It made them feel. And when all was said and done, the ad worked wonders for motivating our target investors to take action investing in the stock. By the end of the campaign, our client's stock had increased by 15%. It outperformed the Nasdaq 11 out of 17 days of our campaign, and the company had 174% *more* investors that bought more than 500 shares (compared to previous quarters). Our client saw a $34.8 million increase of market capitalization in less than 3 weeks. The 5 steps *worked*.

Your marketing strategy is made up of a lot of different tactics: audience targeting, platforms, message. But in the end, it all comes back to one thing—using data to find out what will motivate your customers. Every element of your strategy should be informed by what your customers value and how they behave.

HERE IS WHY YOU HAVE TO BE ADAPTABLE

I could talk about individual tactics until I'm blue in the face. Trust me, after spending more than 20 years in the marketing world, I've tried them all.

Television, radio, postal mail, email, social media? Yep, yep, yep, yep, and yep.

I've worked for B2B, B2C, e-commerce, big, small, privately owned, publicly traded—every kind of company you can imagine. And I've also targeted ads to pretty much every type of customer, client, and politician you can imagine.

I've seen it all.

So, what nugget of wisdom do I have for you? What *indispensable* tactic am I going to tell you your company needs right this instant?

None.

Why? Because there's no magic marketing wand. There's no one-size-fits-all solution. There is no tactic that works for every business, client, or customer. And if your marketing agency tells you otherwise, they're lying to your face.

Look, I know I've given marketers a hard time in this book and in *Fire Them Now*, but when it comes to tactics, a lot of them deserve it. Some marketers just put ads in the same reliable places, no matter who their client is. Have a B2B business? Focus on Google! B2C? Try Google! That approach is like telling every customer at a restaurant to order chicken and waffles, regardless of whether they're diabetic or vegetarian.

Here's the truth. I love tactics, but *they have to fit into your marketing strategy*. We all use tactics, and in fact, at the end of the book, I'll give you a list of 20 different tactics you can try, if they're right for your business. I'm not anti-tactic, as long as you know how and why you're using them.

I've heard from so many business owners, "Why do we need a strategy? I don't see the point. Why can't we just make some ads and run them?" The best way I can answer those questions is with a brief story. It comes from the TV show *Yellowstone*.

In one brilliant scene, John Dutton (played by Kevin Costner) is talking to his son Kayce. He says, "I'd like to believe there's a plan for it all, but I don't see the plan."

Kayce responds, "That's because we're inside of it."

When I saw that, I said, "Oh my God. That's it. That's exactly why so many business owners can't see the value of a data-backed marketing strategy. They're too close to their business, and they've been using tactics-based marketing for so long, they've lost sight of the forest for the trees!"

Look, I'm not pointing fingers here. I can honestly say that I've done the same thing for my personal brand. For a long time, there was no strategy. It was all tactical. I was so inside my own brand that I hadn't realized I wasn't practicing what I preach. I played whack-a-mole instead of being more thoughtful about my over-arching goals and how they align with what my clients want and need. Then I woke up and shifted to a strategic approach, and more success followed quickly.

Your business is too important for a whack-a-mole approach. Every tactic you use should be part of a larger strategic plan. And that strategic plan should always be informed by your own version of the Customer Insights Report. Where do your customers or clients go to look for information? Credibility? Like-minded values? What social media sites do they interact with? And—here's the kicker—how are they changing their media consumption habits over time? Because, trust me, they are changing constantly.

I'll talk more in future chapters about how you can stay on top of changing data, but for now, I want to drive home why you need a strategy that accommodates what your customer/client data says so you can adapt to changing customer preferences.

For example, I worked with a client in the educational industry who wanted to enroll more students in their schools. We spent 5 years marketing this client to parents, and every year, we set our sights on increasing lead generations and conversions in their target market: low-income families in large metropolitan regions of Louisiana.

The data we gathered in our Customer Insights Report each year helped us figure out which channels would be most effective for reaching these moms and dads. Our strategy focused on advertising across several types of platforms, so parents would see and feel our client's messaging multiple times.

Imagine. You're a busy mom or dad on your way to work. You're stuck in traffic, and you hear an ad about an educational opportunity that you think might be a good fit for your kid. Great.

But is that message going to stick in your head once you get to work, start your busy day, and switch gears between clients, phone calls, and emails dozens of times? Probably not. Remember what I said about seeing 10,000 ads per day? If you're thinking about anything kid-related at all, it's about pick-up time, childcare, dinner, or your plans for the evening. You're not thinking about that great after-school program you heard about on the radio.

You head home, get dinner on the table, help with homework, play with the kids, and manage to get them into bed at a reasonable hour. Finally, you have an hour or 2 to yourself. So you hop on social media. Then, there it is! At the top of your social media feed, you see an ad for that same educational opportunity. Now it might start to stick. You might even click through.

Then you walk out to your mailbox to pick up the physical mail and boom! There it is again. The more times—and ways—you can get your potential customers' attention, the better your chance at hooking them and breaking through the 10,000-ads-per-day clutter.

In this particular case, our data showed that our strongest platforms were Facebook ads that drove parents to the school's application form. We also used a "digital mail chase" program, which meant that parents we targeted with online ads were simultaneously "chased" by the marketing we sent through physical mail. Those "2 bites of the apple" led to a 20% higher conversion rate for new student enrollment.

For 3 of the 5 years we worked with this client, our data also showed that radio ads would be effective to supplement our preexisting online marketing ad spend.

But here's the thing. More media isn't always better. Over the lifespan of the whole campaign, we noticed a surprising trend. In the years when we didn't use radio ads, physical mail was much more effective. But in the years when our data suggested radio ads were going to work, the effectiveness of physical mail dropped sharply.

These consumers were changing their media consumption habits routinely, and we had to create an evolving strategic plan that changed each year.

This wasn't a "hit 'em with every tactic in the book" situation. We wanted to make sure we were taking the *right* bites of the apple. Otherwise, our client would have been spending money on ads that didn't work. They would have spent money on radio ads during years where radio wasn't effective, and they would have poured money into physical mailers during the years where those mailers wouldn't make a difference.

Because we were following the actions of these parents year after year, we knew with laser-like precision how they were spending their time, consuming information, and making decisions. Then we reassessed and readjusted our data-backed strategic marketing plan accordingly.

Overall, our ability to adapt on the fly meant that our client got more leads and an even higher conversion rate, not to mention a much lower cost per conversion. Between Year 1 and Year 5, our client saw a jump from 8,199 applications to 12,542 applications. And—here's where it gets really interesting—their price per conversion plummeted from $45 in Year 1 to $18.58 by Year 5.

Your marketing must be adaptable. If you aren't willing and able to evolve your strategy, you will spend *more* for worse results. I don't have to tell you that's bad business.

Step 2 of the Undefeated Marketing System is coming up with a data-backed, unbeatable strategy. But that strategy will never be set in stone forever. Customers are always evolving, which means that your data is always changing. And when the data changes, your strategy needs to follow suit.

How often? When I work with a client, we reevaluate the customer/client data and the strategic roadmap every quarter or every 6 months.

Our education client prioritized adaptability, and they put the parents (customers) at the center of every platform shift they made. They didn't move to digital ads because everyone else was doing it. They listened to their data and built a flexible, cross-platform strategy that perfectly suited their needs—and their customers' needs. And the marketing delivered a huge win for them (and continues to do so).

HERE'S HOW TO BUILD STRONGER TRUST WITH YOUR CUSTOMER

I didn't always know how to come up with this undefeated strategy.

In fact, I struggled for years when I was a kid. I was told that I was dumb and lazy. In middle and high school, I was put in classes that were considered below average and left to rot.

When I was 16, I was finally diagnosed with attention deficit disorder (ADD). It's fairly common today, but I was in the first generation of kids who got that diagnosis, before the medical term changed to attention deficit hyperactivity disorder (ADHD).

For years, I was picked on and bullied. I had been told by teachers and peers that I was incapable or stupid, when really, my brain just didn't conform to the rules of our public education system. But when I got my diagnosis, for the first time in my life, I started to realize that there was nothing wrong with me; my brain just worked differently. Medication helped me cope with the day-to-day, while I also came to the realization that I should only focus on things I was really passionate about.

And I was really passionate about politics, even as a teenager. Later, when I was a political marketer, I was so passionate, I usually worked 7 days a week. There was a 3-year period when I was running political campaigns where I only took 22 days off, *total*. I had a purpose guiding me along.

Since then, I've learned that my ADD is actually a superpower for being an entrepreneur. You move fast, you move forward, and you break things to win. My attention can be on 30 different things, and I never get stressed out over having too much on my plate.

So, by the time I started my corporate marketing company, I thought I had a clear path to success. I had overcome my adolescent struggles and learned how to channel my passions into victory. I knew how to get politicians elected, which, honestly, is 1 of the toughest sells out there. And I had already built a successful, multimillion-dollar political marketing agency.

What could stop me from building a successful corporate marketing company? *Marketing a business is no different from marketing a politician. In fact, it's a lot easier*, I thought.

I still think that—politicians *are* a tougher sell than products or services—but I now know that my "clear path to success" was laced with a serious dose of shortsightedness. During our corporate marketing business's first year, when I hadn't fully developed the Undefeated Marketing System, I made some grave mistakes. By far, the worst day was when a client fired me. We were working for a huge e-commerce food and supplement company that was doing about $75 million in annual sales. Before we listened to his needs or looked at his customer data, we threw a ton of ideas at him, expecting him to be excited.

The guy looked at us like *You clearly don't understand how my company works.* He hated everything we pitched, and when we finished the meeting, he said, "All right, I'll talk to y'all next week."

Then he ghosted us. And I mean *ghosted.* Like, no call, no email, nothing. To this day, I've never heard from him. It killed me. It was a huge client, and I wanted to crush it for him. I spent so many sleepless nights wondering, *Where am I going wrong?*

It was the worst professional year of my life. Do you know the saying "If you want to take the island, burn your boats?" Well, I had burned my boats. I had recently handed over CEO duties at my political marketing company to my partner and created my corporate marketing agency. It's not like I could go back to the political marketing agency and say, "Hey, the corporate marketing company didn't work out. Let me be CEO of the political agency again."

I knew I had to make my business work, but I didn't have a good handle on the problem yet. We had all these great ideas, we knew what we were doing, and we knew how to grow businesses, but something just wasn't right. So I literally locked myself in my office for 3 days and started asking questions. *What do we do that makes us so successful at getting politicians elected and helping other businesses grow? What are the steps we follow to make that happen? How can I make this more systematic?*

And that's when it hit me. I had a huge epiphany and started mapping it all out. *Oh! This is it. We do these 5 steps every single time we market politicians.*

Political marketers inherently follow this 5-step system, but it had never been spelled out. But once I spelled it out and had those 5 steps on a piece of paper in front of me, it clicked. I realized that the problems we'd been having—why our valued client ghosted us and why it had been such a god-awful year—had nothing to do with our clients and everything to do with how I was approaching them. I wasn't listening to them. I was just communicating my ideas. There was nothing systematic about what we were doing *at all.*

Every failure boiled down to one thing: we were more focused on doing it our way (tactics) than on aligning the businesses' outcomes with the customers' needs (strategy). All too often, we were bending to our clients' expectations. When they came to us and said, "We need a YouTube ad," we said, "Sure!" Not once did we stop and say, "Hold on, before we spend your money, where are your customers? How do they consume media?" We were just trying to keep people happy instead of following the 5-step marketing system that had worked so well since the 2004 presidential campaign.

Talk about a "come to Jesus" moment. I knew, right then, that we had to stop trying to appease every business owner's whims, and instead, we had to follow the system that I knew would *always* work for clients. I put my foot down and told myself, "We're the experts. We know how to market businesses, so why aren't we doing it the way we know how? Let's stop trying to satisfy everyone with Band-Aids and develop something that eliminates their risk and that has proven success behind it. And if the client doesn't want their risk eliminated, then we won't work for them."

To achieve all of that, I had to follow my own 5-step system. I had to look at who my clients were, what they wanted, and what was going to help them become successful. Before I could build my own explosive business, I had to meet my clients' strategic needs. Not just their superficial tactical needs like YouTube ads. But their *real* needs. Long-term growth. Lowered risk. I knew that the only way it would work was if I could listen to the business owners' outcomes and also get them to trust my system.

I've said it once, twice, a dozen times—your strategy will hinge entirely upon what your customer wants. Not just what you want to tell them.

But don't worry. I'm not leaving you empty-handed. Because there *is* 1 thing that every marketing strategy should take into account. No matter who you are, what your business is, or who you're speaking to, you will need it.

That 1 thing is trust.

I'll say it again. Every business needs its customers or clients to trust them.

It sounds so obvious, but guess what? Your marketing must *earn* the customer's trust. You can't demand it.

When I started Win BIG Media, I demanded trust from my clients. I said, "Political marketing is the most innovative marketing out there, so trust me and try it." That got me some interested clients, but not committed ones.

If you want your client or customer to commit to you, you can't just tell them to trust you. You have to earn their trust by delivering a great experience and an exceptional product or service.

That's why I reoriented my entire business model around earning trust. How did I shift? Unlike most marketing agencies, we don't require clients to sign long-term contracts. Every client that works with me gets a month-to-month contract. This forces us to prove ourselves day in and day out. My ass is on the line to produce results every month, so we're forced to do everything within the best interest of the client. Their needs always come first.

Just like political marketing, Win BIG's business model is win-or-die. Because if we screw up, we're not going to have a job. That puts the client's priorities before my bottom-line growth.

We also have a massive onboarding system for new clients. During Step 2, where we write a strategic marketing plan for them, we spend hours on the phone with our client just to make sure we're clear about their hopes, desires, and anticipated outcomes. Above all, we're focused on finding out how their interests align with those of their customers and clients.

I'm not going to lie; it can be tedious and a little overwhelming. But we do it because we realize, *We don't know our clients' businesses like they do.* If we want our clients to grow, we have to come together and match the business owners' outcomes with what the customer data is telling us. That's the only way to put together a strategy that will eliminate risk and help them grow their business. And it allows our clients to trust us.

These same considerations apply to your business. If you want your marketing to earn trust, think about the messages you send your customers. Are you demanding their trust? Are you just asserting, "We're the best! Try us!" Are you randomly hitting every social media platform possible with ads and relying on a "spray and pray" mentality?

Or are you following the data and building a data-backed strategic marketing plan that's earning your customers' trust? Are you focusing on where your customers spend their time, understanding what their habits and values are, and speaking to them in a way that's going to make them put their hard-earned money into your business?

Your customers don't want to be told you're the best. They want to feel it.

HERE'S HOW STRATEGY IS EVERYWHERE YOU LOOK

In this chapter, I've mostly focused on marketing strategy, which makes sense, since this is a marketing book. But I'd be doing you a huge disservice if I didn't point out that data-based strategies aren't *just* a marketing tool. They're also useful in other areas of your life.

You don't have to be a political candidate, trial lawyer, doctor, or coach to get value out of the 5-step formula. You can use it to stay flexible, responsive, and strategic in your everyday life. My wife and I have gotten so reliant on the 5 steps, we even used them to make decisions about our daughter's education.

My daughter has my brain. She's super creative, so a few years ago, she hit a wall with her public school. I don't want to get too into the weeds about how much she struggled. But let's just say that school drop-off time was the most dreaded part of her day.

I understood her angst, and that was enough data for us. It was clear that her public school wasn't teaching her in a way that worked for her brain. So we talked to our daughter and gathered even more data about her experience, what she wanted, and what she didn't want in a school (Step 1). Then my wife and I sat down and came up with a strategy for finding a school that would work (Step 2), based on all the data we had gathered about what, specifically, our daughter needed.

We followed our strategy and talked to everyone who had experience with Montessori schools, alternative schools, and private schools. We came up with a list of schools that seemed to fit, and we found out even more about how they were run. We picked a short list of schools that fit our family's brand: love and creativity (Step 3).

Then we tested (Step 4). We sent her on a shadow day at our top pick, and when we picked her up that afternoon, she said, "This is where I'm going to school." I said, "Are you sure? What about your friends at your old school? You don't know anyone here." And she said, "I don't care. I want to go here." And let me tell you, when your 6-year-old is that clear on the decision, you listen. It was clear that this school made her feel empowered.

We made the decision to launch and enroll her in that school (Step 5). And it's been the greatest decision we've ever made. She takes art classes, plays in a rock and roll band, and goes to a school whose mission is all about love, acceptance, and creativity. All the kids have their own laptops, and instead of using desks, they sit on sofas. Some people may roll their eyes, and of course, her school wouldn't work for everyone. But it works perfectly for my daughter. Now she's actually excited to go to school every day.

When our daughter was miserable, it would have been easy to try a lot of new tactics. We could have hired tutors, signed her up for after-school activities, and talked to her teachers about ways they could help. Some of those tactics might have eased the problem, but they wouldn't have solved it.

In most cases, tactics aren't enough. You need a strategy. You need to see the big picture. You need to have a clear, data-supported plan. Whether you're running a political campaign, growing a business, or nurturing your child, a definable game plan is the best tool you've got for eliminating risk and finding solutions that work.

UTILIZING YOUR MARKETING TACTICS IS SECONDARY

Imagine this: you're a Republican candidate facing one of the toughest congressional races in the country. You've got a blue-leaning city in your district, and your opponent is a full-time grassroots candidate with a remarkable ability to raise money. But on election night, you're almost entirely stress-free. Why? Because your marketing campaign gave you such a solid edge that you don't really have to worry about losing.

That story doesn't sound very likely, but that's exactly what happened to Roger Williams. He didn't just win a tight race. He soared to victory with a comfortable margin.

The reason that was possible was because his campaign followed a data-backed strategic marketing plan to the letter. We knew exactly what would resonate with voters, and that helped us figure out how we could deliver that message in the best possible way and get Roger's supporters to the polls.

Your strategic marketing plan should always be informed by the data you collected in Step 1. It's useless to put an ad on a platform that won't reach your target audience. As you consider budget, timeline, audience, message, media, and platform, make sure you're taking your customers' values and behaviors into account.

Once you understand what motivates your customers, you can come up with a plan for effectively speaking to those motivations that align with your outcomes. And once you have a data-backed strategic marketing plan, then—and only then—you can start creating (or recreating) a brand that will move them to conversions.

CHAPTER 4

STEP 3: CREATE YOUR DATA-BACKED MESSAGING AND CREATIVE BRAND (OR REBRAND)

"ON MARCH 1, YOUR CHOICE COULD RESET EVERYTHING."

If you're a voter who's completely dissatisfied with the way your government is being run, there are no more powerful words. A "reset" is a promise for a fresh start. It's an opportunity. And voters were being told, *You have the power to make it happen.*

Those words may have been simple, but they packed a punch. And sure enough, on March 1, when Minnesotan Republicans went to the polls, they were determined to get their reset. They were determined to put the candidate who offered them a "reset" into office. That candidate was Marco Rubio.

Minnesotan Republicans made their choice loud and clear. On

March 1, Marco Rubio won the 2016 Minnesota Republican presidential caucus by a landslide. Out of 114,254 votes cast, Rubio came out with 41,397. That's 36.24% of the vote—*miles* ahead of the third-place choice, Donald Trump, who only had 21.42% of the vote.

Of course, we all know that Marco Rubio didn't walk away with the 2016 Republican presidential nomination. In fact, he didn't come close. He didn't even win another state. But the fact remains, he *crushed* that primary in Minnesota, and it's worth asking why.

What helped Rubio rise to the top of such a crowded pack of candidates? What helped the underdog clinch such a major win?

One thing: his brand.

Marco Rubio delivered *exactly* the message that Minnesotans wanted to hear, in *exactly* the way they wanted to hear it.

And the only reason that was possible was because Rubio's brand in Minnesota was based on a deep understanding of what voters wanted and a strategy that took those desires, values, and needs into account and turned them into an emotional choice.

I know this because my firm had a hand in creating that brand. Going into Super Tuesday, Rubio was lagging behind in key states. A super PAC that supported Marco Rubio reached out to us to see if we could help Rubio pick off a win in Minnesota.

It was late in the game, but Rubio was a credible candidate. They hoped that a solid win in Minnesota would put some wind in his sails and help him gain momentum.

So, first things first, we created a Voter Insights Report, the political version of the Customer Insights Report (Step 1). Based on millions of data points, we learned that the number 1 thing Minnesota Republican caucus voters wanted was *change*. We also learned that they were really worried about national security issues, and they favored authentically conservative candidates.

Based on that information, we developed a strategy (Step 2) that would allow us to target the exact voters we needed to win the state, and we created ads that reinforced our voter insights research, *down to the very last detail.*

One of the most important pieces of content we created was a video ad that incorporated voters' must-have motivators. The first 5 seconds of the video focused on the magic words: *Your choice could reset everything.* White text. Black background. Booming movie-guy voice-over. Major emphasis. There was no getting away from that message. If you wanted change, this would get your attention. Everything about it screamed, *Here's your chance for transformation.*

You might think that we'd jump straight into Rubio's campaign— who he was, what he stood for, what changes he wanted to make. But we knew that wasn't revolutionary enough. It wouldn't stir up the emotional fires of our target voters.

Instead, we used our ads to dig deep into the themes of national security and conservative values, the other 2 issues that Minnesota voters cared so much about. We went negative (see Chapter 8 and *Fire Them Now*), highlighting everything that we knew drove Republican caucus voters crazy: Speaker Nancy Pelosi, Hillary Clinton, and Barack Obama.

We flashed a quick succession of clips that spoke directly to those voters' frustrations and fears: Clinton testifying in front of Congress, Iran's leader denouncing America, raging wildfires, Pelosi cackling, and Obama saying, "If you like your plan, you can keep your plan."

Flash. Flash. Flash. One hot touchpoint after another.

By the time we were 16 seconds into our ad, our targeted viewers had seen every indignity they despised. And we hadn't said Marco Rubio's name or shown his image *at all*.

Then, cut back to black. Enter white text and booming voice with a message: "Only one conservative choice for president can do it."

Finally, at the very end of the ad, voters saw Marco Rubio speaking passionately and authoritatively about national defense. The last 8 seconds of that ad were all about branding Rubio's strength. He was a *conservative* leader prepared to *defend the country* and *make change*.

The ad successfully stressed voters' core motivators, but that's not all it did. It packed a double punch because it also addressed a shortcoming we saw in every other Republican's messaging.

Every other campaign was telling candidates, "You need to attack your opponents," and everyone in the Republican primary was out there beating up on each other. They were slinging mud and trading insults like kindergartners.

If you know my work, you know I love a good comparison ad—a negative ad—done right. But the voter data was clear. Our main opponents, Cruz and Trump, were hurting themselves by attacking each other and other Republicans.

Our testing (Step 4) showed that our ads going negative against Democratic leadership rather than our Republican opponents would engage swing voters toward Rubio's corner. Our testing showed that Republican voters in Minnesota didn't really care which Republican could "out-Republican" all the other candidates. They were way more concerned about shaking things up with the Democrats in Washington.

So we didn't attack any other Republican candidates. We created a brand for Rubio that attacked the status quo of the last 8 years. And that made our message stand out when we launched (Step 5).

While other candidates spent their time showing how different they were from each other, we spent our time showing how Rubio was different from Democrats. We didn't waste time branding Donald Trump, Ted Cruz, or other Republican options. Instead, we branded voters' top problems and showed that Rubio was the solution.

Rubio may not have won the party nomination, but after launching our campaign (Step 5), a good brand helped him clinch a significant Republican primary caucus. And he even beat Donald Trump by 16,924 votes.

Take a page out of Rubio's book. Your brand should be markedly different from your competition's and based on connecting with your customers and clients. The reason Rubio resonated so strongly with Minnesota voters was because he (and his brand) made a connection with the leadership and issues they cared about.

YOUR BRAND ISN'T BUILT ON 1-SIDED WINS

The following happens to me on an almost-daily basis: someone I don't know reaches out to me on LinkedIn through a direct message, and all they do is pitch me to give them money. *Hey, we have a similar connection. Did you know I have a product you should try? I can give you a free demo!*

No, I don't want a demo of your product. I'm busy.

I'll bet 99 times out of 100—no, 999 times out of 1,000—those pitches don't go anywhere. In fact, they're actually hurting business. That's because *no relationship should start with asking for a handout.*

Stop sending business proposals where *you* win first. If you really want to build a great brand and sell your products or services, you have to earn trust, build a relationship, and forge a partnership. *When the other side wins first*—and only then—do you win. If you try to skip steps, you're just going to come off as a shallow person out for your own gain. Plus, it's just a better way to live your life. Give first.

Want to know when I've been most impressed from a cold

outreach to me? When people have reached out to offer me something *for my gain* instead of cutting straight to their own win.

For example, when my book *Fire Them Now* came out, a guy reached out to me and offered me $5,000 for jumping on a 1-hour call. I thought, *Dang, that guy is serious!* Another person reached out and said, "Can I ask you a few questions? I'll buy 250 books." A third one reached out to me said, "Would you talk to my team on the phone about your book? I'd like to make a 5-figure contribution to your favorite charity." I immediately responded to all those offers, and all of those people are still friends today. Plus, they've probably made more money off me than I received from them.

Those kinds of gestures show that people really want to build a relationship. They're seeking a connection, not some self-interested payoff.

Of course, by the time we were done talking, I had hopefully given them some useful advice, but here's the key: they weren't asking me to do it for free. They respected my time, and because of that, I respected them even more.

If you want to move fast on building a brand, do things to help people. Building personal connections and giving first is always the best way to market your business.

Now, there are better and worse ways to do that. The methods I described above count as some of the "better" ones. Here's an example of "worse." One influential woman who was in the national news media sent me a message to say she had been moved by my health story and felt compelled by God to reach out to me. At the end of the note, she invited me to come have dinner at her house with her family.

Don't get me wrong—her email was perfectly nice. But this was the wrong way to make a connection. I'm a father with a young child, and I don't have 3 spare hours to spend on dinner with a stranger. I just don't. And the fact that this hadn't occurred to her showed me that she wasn't really thinking about the other person in the situation (me). She was thinking about what would be fun, interesting, and convenient for herself. She wanted to steal my time.

Every element of your brand is built on cultivating relationships, and relationships aren't about 1-sided wins. Take your time and build them the right way. That lasts a lifetime. Focus on what the customer wants and needs. Follow the same steps you would with any other relationship in your life, and do it in the order I discuss in this book.

Think of it like dating. Just because you found the man or woman of your dreams, it doesn't mean you should propose on the first date. That *definitely* won't get you the results you want. But it will get you rejected.

Or think of it like a friendship. Just because you recently found a friend you connect with, it doesn't mean you should treat them like someone you've known for 20 years.

The same goes for your brand. You can't skip ahead in building the relationship. You can't run up to new customers and say, "Hey,

I saw some data, and I know what you like. Will you buy my product and be loyal to me for the rest of your life?" without looking like you've lost your marbles.

Even if you've got the best brand in the world, you have to take time to focus on what your customers like, cultivate a connection, and build that connection based on where your brand has alignment with them.

YOUR BRAND IS LIKE A PIZZA

I just explained why you can't skip steps when you're building a relationship with your brand, but most corporate marketing agencies skip steps for their clients like there's no tomorrow.

When a typical marketing agency gets a new client, they usually leap straight into rebranding and content creation, and push a "brand first, conversion second" mentality. That's good for the agency's bottom line, but it's terrible for the client. I talked about this approach in *Fire Them Now* and showed how the "If you brand it, they will come" mentality is one of corporate marketing's biggest lies.

I don't want to downplay branding's importance. Having a successful brand is essential to having a successful business. But there's a formula to creating a great brand that works every time. You don't just whip a brand up out of thin air and send it into the world.

Just think of the iconic clothing brand Supreme. In 2020, they were sold to VF Corporation in an all-cash deal for $2.1 billion.

Do you think they just pulled their brand out of thin air? Do you think they said, "We'll make a cool logo, stick it on everything, and people will come"?

No. The brand started in 1994 as a skateboarding lifestyle brand, and they strategically targeted youth subcultures. They collaborated with cutting-edge designers, artists, and musicians. Their iconic red-and-white logo was based on propaganda art. Raving fans line up outside their brick-and-mortar stores for hours just to buy a T-shirt.

Every single aspect of Supreme's devil-may-care brand was built around their relationship with rebellious youth. Even the fact that they could charge sky-high prices for basic clothing like hoodies and T-shirts seemed like part of their "F*** you" attitude.

Brands like Supreme don't happen by chance. They happen because someone (unconsciously) tapped into the Undefeated Marketing System and knew that developing a great brand was a multistep process.

First, you have to find out what your customers or clients want. Second, you need to strategically align their values with your company's own desired outcomes. Then you can use that alignment to build a great brand. In other words, you have to go through steps 1 and 2 before you can brand (or rebrand) your marketing.

Remember that story about how political marketers find alignment between voters and candidates? Smart political candidates don't talk about 20 issues they support. They campaign on 2 to 3 issues that they support and their voters want as their top issues.

When you run a marketing campaign, your first goal is to move your customer or client from simply *recognizing* your ad to *discovering* your products or services. Once they've clicked through to your site (discovery), they're going to engage with your brand. Your brand has to reinforce all the things you learned about your customers/clients from your Step 1 data deep dive if you want it to appeal to them on a deep level.

The more your brand engages your customer, the deeper your relationship with that customer will be. Think about how much attention and money major brands like Starbucks pour into their existing customer relationships. Do you think Double Star Day incentives, convenient app-based ordering, and reusable, branded travel mugs are designed to appeal to first-time customers? No. Those are for the die-hard Starbucks-goers who keep coming back, rain or shine.

Starbucks isn't doing this to convert new customers. They're trying to deepen the relationships they already have. And why do they do that? Because the lifetime value they can gain from those customers is *huge*.

So let me ask you, what's preventing you from following their branding lead? What's stopping you from marketing to your current customers and increasing their lifetime buying value to your company?

I can only give you this advice because I've been on the other side of the equation. A few years ago, I screwed this up, and it's a great example of how you *shouldn't* build a brand.

Remember the pest control company I mentioned in Chapter 1? Over the course of our Undefeated Marketing System, we doubled their conversions, and word of that success got around in the pest control world. So we were approached by a noncompeting startup pest control company. Their sales had screeched to a halt, and they had no idea how to get their operation running smoothly again.

The owners told me, "We already knew you had a lot of success with your national pest control client. Then we heard you on Peter Diamandis's podcast, and we knew we had to shift gears if we wanted to grow our bottom line. We want to get on board quick."

I saw the potential for a great company. The owners had all the right intentions, and they were authentic and passionate about their work. I liked these guys, and I really wanted to help. So I reluctantly agreed to work with them and bypass the full 5-step system. *Red alert. Mayday.* That was my first mistake.

We followed Step 1 and got a thorough handle on who their customers were, what they wanted, and what they cared about. But they wanted to go fast and speed up the campaign. Before writing a strategic plan (Step 2), we started creating and running ads. Mistake number 2.

It wasn't until then that my team alerted me to their website (brand), and I realized the error of my ways. The first words out of my mouth when I looked at their site were "Holy shit, this is bad." It was wall-to-wall text, and my eyes just hurt looking at it. I wanted to see an image, *any image*, just to break it up.

Be careful what you wish for.

When I scrolled down on the home page, I got an image, all right. There was a sloppy picture of the 2 owners, wearing random T-shirts, casually leaning on a car. It looked more like a profile pic on a dating site than the lead promotional image for a trust-worthy pest control company. (Actually, to be completely honest, I don't even think it would have worked for a dating site. No one in their right mind would have wanted to swipe right. I love these guys, but seriously, it was that bad.)

There was nothing about that picture that made you feel, *It's a great idea to invite these guys into my home to spray bug spray around my kids and pets.* It was totally unprofessional.

To add insult to injury, the website was *not* mobile-friendly. If you pulled it up on your phone, you couldn't see all the text, the images were cut off, and nothing was the right size.

You might say, "Who cares if the images didn't look good on an iPhone?"

According to Google Analytics, 52% of customers, that's who. Yes, 52% of customers say that a bad mobile experience made them less likely to engage with a company, while 48% report that they feel frustrated and annoyed by websites that aren't mobile-friendly.

Losing the immediate trust of *half* of the market when you're trying to grow your business is a problem. That's a whole lot of potential customers to annoy.

But it also gets worse. Remember this gem of a stat from Chapter 1? According to Compuware, a single bad experience on a website makes users *88%* less likely to visit the website again.

I'm repeating that number to let it sink in. You've got one shot to reach your potential customers. If your website bugs them, they won't ever return. That's how important your brand is to the customer.

That god-awful abomination of a website had to go. Otherwise, this company didn't have an ice cube's chance in hell of getting the returns they wanted.

Like any good marketing agency, we were honest. We told them, "This isn't going to work. Your brand is completely off, and your website needs an overhaul."

"Oh, we know," they replied. "We're fixing it right now. Let's just run the ads. By the time they run and leads come in the door, we'll have this fixed. We promise the website will be good to go."

They were on a tight budget, so I understood why they wanted to do the work themselves. I assumed, *They have the data, and they know their site's a mess,* and I took them at their word. I trusted they'd build a site that matched the new messaging.

That was my third mistake.

Our initial ads ended up generating 237 leads in the first week. 237 potential customers saw our ads and clicked this pest control company's website to inquire about hiring them. That's *triple* what they had before they hired us. But out of all those leads, they only got 8 conversions.

Naturally, they were disappointed. We had come up with a fool-proof plan, and it had still flopped. They asked, "What was wrong with our messaging?"

Honestly, we were as baffled as they were. Those numbers just didn't make sense.

So we went back and looked at where things fell apart. Immediately, we realized that *nothing* was wrong with the messaging. The problem was with their brand.

And, to be more exact, can you guess what their biggest brand problem was?

That friggin' website. They hadn't changed it!

When customers saw the new data-backed ads, they responded positively. They decided to give the company a shot and learn more about them and their offer. So they clicked through and *bam!* They were socked with an untrustworthy website with illegible text and 2 dudes in T-shirts. No wonder almost no one signed up for their services!

Our data showed that customers wanted trust, safety, and local ownership in their pest control services. Those selling points were *all over* the ads we created for this company. The first thing customers saw were messages like "Safe," "Effective," "Locally owned," "Pet- and family-safe products," and "No-contact service." That's why they got so many leads.

But on the website? Those values were nowhere to be found. The brand was announcing "We're incompetent," not "You can trust us to take care of your loved ones."

That messy website might as well have had 2 simple words at the top: "Run Away."

Remember, when people search for a pest control company, their first priority is "I want those bugs killed." They'll usually look into the top 3 results, and out of those, they'll choose the 1 that stands out. That's when a pest control company needs to show their "difference that makes the difference" to have them stand out from the competition.

In the case of our national pest control company client, the "difference that made the difference" was the fact that they were a family-owned company with a commitment to community improvement and using green products. Everything on their website advertised quality and professionalism. There were no guys in T-shirts; there were customer service technicians in uniforms. People coming to the site immediately knew that they could trust the company to serve their needs and keep their family safe.

That national pest control company built an *entire brand* around their data-backed message. They followed all 5 steps, and in return, they got exceptional results. They hit an all-times sales record after hiring us.

Our second pest control client, on the other hand, didn't follow through. They only tackled one part of their brand, not the whole shebang. And let me tell you, the rest of the shebang needed work.

These clients didn't understand one crucial thing: your brand is like a pizza. One slice may be the data-backed messaging in a video ad; another slice may be how your brand looks on the website. Another slice is about telling your authentic story. Every element of your company's brand makes up another slice, until eventually, you have a whole pie.

Your brand has to take every slice into account. Otherwise, customers aren't going to eat your pizza. They'll order from an entirely different pizza joint.

And who can blame them? Stop for a minute and imagine you've ordered a pizza. The delivery man shows up, hands you the piping hot box, and you can smell that delicious pizza smell coming from inside. You lift the lid to peek, and the side closest to you looks incredible. It's gooey and cheesy, with steam rising from the top.

You carry the pizza inside, set it on the dining room table, and throw back the lid—only to notice that one slice is missing.

I guarantee you won't eat that pizza. You'll call the Better Business Bureau or the health department.

That's the mistake this startup made (and that I made by not demanding that they follow the 5-step Undefeated Marketing System). They had the right messaging, but their brand's pizza had a big slice missing.

Take my advice: you can't skip steps or cut corners and still expect people to buy your brand or be brand loyal. Building a great brand is all about consistency. Every slice needs to speak to your customers' needs and wants and fit perfectly within your overall data-backed strategy.

YOUR SUCCESS IS BASED ON YOUR CONNECTION WITH CUSTOMERS

Let me tell you one of the best branding stories I've ever heard. John Truchard is a lifelong winemaker in Napa Valley. His high-end wine, named John Anthony Vineyards, was established over 20 years ago with blood, sweat, and tears. It became successful and very profitable.

That wasn't easy. Because let me tell you, making and selling wine in California is *hard*. The supply chain is massive, and the distribution roadblocks are endless. You also have to take into account the onerous regulations and taxes that all California business owners endure. And that's before any economic disruptions or natural disasters have entered the picture.

So, when I say that John Truchard built a successful, highly profitable wine business, that means he overcame the odds. John Truchard is a unicorn in the wine business.

But, of course, disruption happens—even for unicorns. The Great

Recession hit, and while John Anthony Vineyards survived (and is still making delicious high-end wines), it was also a wake-up call for John and his wife, Michele.

What do most entrepreneurs do in tough, challenging times? They get scrappy and innovative, and create opportunities—and that's what John and Michele did. And how did they do it? They put a lot of thought into how they could make a deeper connection with their customers.

They dug into their customer insights data (Step 1), and they noticed that California chardonnay drinkers love the buttery taste of chardonnay. In a contest between "buttery" and "minerally" wine, buttery is the choice for average wine drinkers. They knew that was their key to their customers' palates, hearts—and ultimately, wallets.

Next, they came up with a strategic plan (Step 2). John and Michele are the creators and majority owners of JaM Cellars, and they planned to create a buttery chardonnay as their signature wine. Instead of buying a vineyard and growing their own chardonnay grapes, they decided to buy high-end grapes produced by other winemakers. That way, they could avoid the hefty costs that go into cultivating, growing, and picking grapes. But they could still achieve their ultimate goal: to create the butteriest chardonnay possible.

They knew that their brand (Step 3) was all about the buttery flavor that their customers loved, so they made a genius decision. They named their chardonnay "Butter." It was brilliant and obvious.

The name is so distinctive that any wine drinker knows exactly what they're getting. If you don't like buttery chardonnay, you'll never buy Butter. If you do, then it's going to be one of the first bottles you pick up. Thus, their brand hits the bull's-eye 100% of the time with its target market.

They tested their brand (Step 4) by putting bottles of Butter in some local stores, and sales immediately exploded. It was evident that customers were going into the grocery store looking for a chardonnay. They knew these wine consumers liked buttery wines, but guess what? There wasn't an easy way to tell which chardonnays would give them the taste they wanted. That is, there wasn't an easy way until John and Michele put Butter on their label and onto the shelf, and it screamed to customers, "This is exactly what you want!"

By the time John and Michele launched their Butter brand (Step 5), they knew that their product was exactly what their customers wanted and that it was going to blow them away. Today, the Truchards are the #1 chardonnay maker in America, and they've created one of the most successful wines in the world.

Do you know why that wine was so successful (aside from being delicious)? Because John and Michele were *connected to their chardonnay-crazed customers*. They knew exactly what they wanted, and they put those desires at the center of every decision they made.

Creating a successful brand is all about understanding what your customers value, coming up with a plan for delivering, and using Step 3—branding—to forge a connection. I want to stress that last word: "connection."

What do I mean when I say, "Having a connection with your customer is crucial?"

Well, in some ways, connection is very simple. It hinges on 1-on-1 human gestures that show a person they matter. When you send your friend a "good luck" text before a job interview, that's a connection. When you buy your spouse's favorite bottle of wine during the weekly grocery run, that's a connection. When you make sure your children's night light is on when you tuck them in, that's a connection.

These are small, basic gestures, but they speak volumes.

When it comes to business, that kind of connection can be hard. When you're barraged with thousands of ads every day, most of those ads won't even register, much less connect with you.

There is no faster way to create customer or client loyalty than forging a genuine, personal connection with them.

In politics, the way we do that is to go door-to-door and meet voters. When I worked with South Dakota's US Senator John Thune, he would wake up every Sunday, get a list of swing voters in his community, and knock on doors to meet them and discuss the issues.

In 2004, Thune ran against US Senate Majority Leader Tom Daschle. Thune knew there was no way he could meet everyone. But every Sunday, no matter what, he knocked on the doors of undecided voters. His goal was to meet as many undecided voters as he could. Thune ended up winning that race and defeating the most powerful incumbent US senator in the country.

Being there face-to-face and letting people know that you care, is the quintessential way to form a connection and build a great brand.

And, by the way, those knocks were more powerful than the numbers might suggest. For every door Thune visited, he got the added bonus of word of mouth. Those people told their friends and family, "This guy running for the United States Senate actually came and knocked on my door." If Thune got the right door, it could lead him to dozens of new voters.

In the corporate world, you're not going to walk door-to-door saying hello to invite everyone to your store. But that doesn't mean you can't get personal. Let me tell you about one brand in particular that blew me away. They were able to create such an instant connection with me that I can't stop raving about them.

Because of my health condition, I have to stick to a very specific diet. One of the things I can't eat anymore is peanut butter. But I *can* eat organic pecan butter. (Yes, there is such a thing, and it is insanely good.)

Over the course of a year, I bought pecan butter from several different companies off Amazon. One of those companies was Guidry Organic Farms, based in Lafayette, Louisiana.

Like anyone who orders anything on Amazon, all I expected was to get a box containing the thing I ordered. Maybe there'd be some bubble wrap and a receipt. But what Amazon purchase comes with additional bells and whistles? Not many.

So imagine my surprise when I received my jar of organic pecan butter, complete with a handwritten note: "We take great pride in our product, and my dad wanted me to tell you that you should put this pecan butter on some vanilla ice cream. It will light your world on fire!"

There I was, picturing some old dad in Louisiana, mixing his pecan butter with ice cream. I was instantly transported, and I thought, *How brilliant is this? A daughter's handwritten note to a stranger, telling me something about her dad. I will never buy pecan butter from another company.*

The best part? It didn't cost them a dime to market personally and authentically that way. To repeat—it's the difference that makes the difference.

This is how every company's marketing should look. Everybody wants human connection, and we're living in a world that doesn't have much of that these days. In the age of "me, me, me," small gestures that show you care go 1,000 times further than any standalone ad could. Great customer service will always win the long game of business.

Here's another example I talked about on entrepreneur Gary Vaynerchuk's podcast. My wife loves the New York fashion designer Billy Reid, and she recently ordered a bunch of clothes from the Billy Reid website. When her package arrived, she noticed that the company had enclosed a handwritten thank-you note from the New York store manager.

She was blown away, and just because of that little personal touch, she will buy clothes from Billy Reid for the rest of her life. A great product plus a great connection equals a great brand.

Guidry and Billy Reid understood the power of a personal thank-you note, but don't think that's the only way to create a personal connection. There are plenty of other things you can do to show your customers and clients you care.

In fact, depending on who your customers and clients are and what they value, other gestures might have more of an impact. That's why I'm a broken record telling you to *always look to your customers' data to understand how they think, what they care about, and how to serve them best*. If you don't know what your customer wants, there's no way to get personal with them.

Let me give you an example of a different kind of connection. We were working with an apparel company, and they wanted to find new ways to connect with their customers. Thanks to the Step 1 deep data dive into their Customer Insights Report, we noticed that the customers who bought their products also shopped at stores like Whole Foods, Starbucks, and Chick-fil-A. What do all of those brands have? Loyalty programs. We also noticed that most of these customers were registered for airline frequent-flyer miles and hotel points programs. So, basically, their customers liked the opportunity to earn points and gain rewards.

Before we came to this conclusion, our clients had been laser-focused on sales. They ate, slept, and breathed conversions. But thanks to our data, we were able to show them that their relationship with customers was about a lot more than sales. It was about building loyalty to the brand. And the best way to do that was through an effective incentives program.

Now it's an integral part of their brand.

Another one of our clients was a B2B real estate title company whose target market was real estate agents. When we dug into their Customer Insights Report, we found something completely unexpected: 72% of the real estate agents in their client database owned dogs.

Would you ever have made the connection between real estate agents and dog-lovers? Probably not.

But it was the perfect opportunity for our client. They already had a policy allowing employees to bring their dogs into the office, and we decided to turn that policy into a selling point.

On the website, we included bio pictures of all the dogs owned by people working at the title company. We made a video of the owners and their story of why they started the company, and the dogs are all in there. We also emphasized the fact that when real estate agents come in for a closing, there will be a bunch of dogs walking around. There's no greater perk for dog lovers.

When this title company came to us for a rebrand, they had no idea that we were going to come back with "dogs" as the answer, but that's exactly what their client loves. And for this title client's specific customers, the dogs were like magic. Nothing could have felt more personal. The connection was totally out of left field, but *it was genuine.* That's the power of a deep data dive.

There are billions of people with phones in front of their faces. Your company is trying to claw through the noise to get a shred of their attention. At the end of the day, if your customer doesn't have a connection with you, your brand is as generic as a can of beans, and you're wasting valuable dollars on your marketing.

The minute your customer sees you as a commodity, your brand is dead.

Why?

Because people don't connect to commodities. They connect to stories. Values. Memories. Emotions.

You want your customers to rave about you, tell all their friends about you, and buy your products over and over. And to make that happen, you have to get personal.

Does your marketing do that? Or are your current and potential new customers just seeing an indistinguishable set of products and services?

Your marketing isn't just about the products or services you can offer customers or clients—it's about the connections you build along the way. That's what's going to keep them coming back for more.

Meet your customers where *they* are, instead of focusing on what *you* want them to hear. You can talk until you're blue in the face about how great you are, but unless they're able to see themselves in your brand, you're wasting your time.

BEING AUTHENTIC WITH YOUR BRAND WILL EXPLODE YOUR SALES

Do you know what made the connection between the title company and dogs so powerful?

It was authentic. The title company already had dogs running around the office. The employees sincerely loved dogs. Dogs were an integral part of the company.

They didn't just read our report and think, *Oh, dogs'll get the job done*, and head to the pound to adopt. They found an authentic, sincere, *genuine* alignment between their interests and those of their client.

"Authentic" is an easy word to toss around, but it's not always easy to live up to. What does it mean to be truly authentic?

It means that when you find an alignment between your business and your customers or clients, you connect it—no matter how "out there," controversial, or nontraditional it seems.

Many companies try to straddle some imaginary play-it-safe fence. They know they need to stand out, but they're scared to be authentic and cutting-edge. They're worried about offending or alienating their customers, instead of staying true to their brand.

Here's a great example currently facing the food industry. The tide is rolling in favor of plant-based foods, and food companies are seeing a massive sea change.

How massive? Virtually every fast-food chain has opted to put plant-based foods on their menus: Burger King, White Castle, KFC, Wendy's, Subway, Carl's Jr., McDonald's...the list goes on and on. But one chain decided to be an outlier. They picked their lane, committed to it, and stayed true to their brand's meat-lover image.

That brand was Arby's.

Not only did they shy away from this wave of plant-based foods, but they also shoved it back in the face of the vegetarian movement with the slogan "We Have the Meats."

Then, they took it one step further...They doubled down by creating a—wait for it—*meat-based carrot*, or as they referred to it, "megetable," or "the Marrot."

Yeah, you read that right. It was a "megetable" made of turkey meat, dyed orange with carrot juice, and shaped into a carrot-like log. Their logic was "If *they* can make meat from veggies, we can make veggies from meat."

Maybe it sounds disgusting to you (it does to me too), but there was a massive population that was sick and tired of the "vegan nanny state" telling them what to do. These customers love meat, and only one company was out there saying, "We have your back. Eat all the meat you want."

I'd bet $100,000 Arby's knew what their customers wanted by investing in customer data before they launched. They found a niche in their data and built an outlier strategy and brand around it.

Arby's campaign for a meat-based vegetable branded them as *the* outlier in the fast-food wars. Article after article focused on the megetable. The belligerent attitude. The unapologetic "meatiness" of it all.

The campaign created a swell of customer loyalty and garnered them at least 8 figures in *free* advertising. It didn't matter how "gross" the Marrot was. Arby's won either way.

If you asked me, "Phillip, what's the one pet peeve you have with business owners these days?" here's what I'd say:

They're afraid of their own marketing shadow. They are not committed. They're afraid to be outliers. They want to be authentic, but they can't go for it. They play it safe because they're paralyzed by the fear of uncertainty.

If you want to be #1 in your industry, you can't win with a fearful, play-it-safe marketing strategy amongst the 10,000 competitors you're facing online every day.

Don't spend your marketing dollars to be like everyone else. Find the unique lane that allows you to still connect with your customers, take a chance, and commit to the strategy. Stand for something, serve your target audience, and hold to your principles. The money will come. It always comes to the truly smart and authentic brands.

Ask yourself this question: How do you want your business to be remembered? For following the status quo in these disruptive times or for trying to create something authentic, original, and honest?

If you commit to being authentic and letting yourself be vulnerable, your customers will probably like you even more.

Perfect is boring. That's a lesson I learned all too well during my time in politics. Voters want candidates they can connect with, not perfect, plastic robots. It's the campaign's job to determine how to authentically tell a candidate's story so their true personality shines through.

Want a good example? I worked on a campaign where our team actually unlocked the candidate's *authentic* brand before anyone else had a clue.

Carlos Lopez-Cantera was the lieutenant governor of Florida, and during his campaign, the people close to him learned that he had a major weakness: doughnuts. And when I say weakness, I mean it. This man loved doughnuts more than anything in this world. Every time he traveled to meet with voters or have constituent meetings, he wanted to stop for doughnuts. Not only that, he always knew just the place to go. The man was a walking encyclopedia of doughnut shops.

Doughnuts were Carlos's kryptonite.

One of Carlos's staffers loved this genuine quirk, so he made a video of Carlos talking about how much he loved doughnuts. In the video he created, you can just see the glimmer in Carlos's eye. He looks like a kid on Christmas morning.

At one point, the staffer asks Carlos, "How many doughnuts have you eaten in a single sitting?" and without missing a beat, Carlos says with a smirk, "Is my wife going to see this?" Guilty pause and a grin. "Probably 6, 7 doughnuts."

Unbeknownst to the lieutenant governor, this video team showed the video in review to his wife (while filming her). Then they spliced in his wife's reaction. The staffer says, "Did you know that Carlos ate over half a dozen doughnuts in one sitting?"

For 3 whole seconds, her face radiates quiet shock, a little eyeroll, and then disappointment. And that's it. That's the whole video.

More importantly, that's good branding. You don't even know what he believes in as a political candidate, but you like him. And if you have a significant other in your life, you know that they would probably do something just like that to you. I know my wife would roll her eyes if she found out I chowed down on that many doughnuts in a day. It connects on so many levels. Of course, no one would vote for him on the basis of that video alone, but it would go a long way toward endearing the voters toward Carlos.

The video is a riot, but it's also a great lesson to you as a business owner and marketer: be authentic, be true to yourself, be willing to be outrageous, and you will build an amazing brand.

THE IMPORTANCE OF VIDEO IN TODAY'S WORLD

I've told you several times that I'm platform agnostic. I don't *always* go for Facebook or Instagram or any other social media platform. Where you place your ads depends entirely on your customer eyeballs.

But let's be clear. I'm *not* agnostic when it comes to the tools of media. You have to use certain kinds of creativity to break through the marketing clutter.

When was the last time you clicked on a banner ad graphic and bought the advertised product? Maybe never.

That's because the world has been optimized for video. We're streaming video at a record amount, and every day, that record grows even more.

If you want to run successful online marketing campaigns, you must use video to tell compelling stories. Let me repeat that again. *You must use video to tell compelling stories.* Every social media and advertising platform has made this decision for you. It's not up for debate. If you don't understand this, you will lose before you even start the game.

A few years ago, Google and Facebook executives sat me and my team down and asked, "What are your growth plans inside your company?" We said, "We want to hire more people to do business development, and we want to hire more client account support."

"No," they said. "You need to build out a video production team. You need to be able to make compelling video content, and you need to do it right now." (To repeat, this was a few years ago, so it's even more true now.)

At the time, that was a terrifying demand. It's not at all what we had intended. But we did it anyway. And we did it because they told us, "The future is going to be video, and if you don't get on board, you're dead."

They were right. Video is crushing every other form of media. According to Wyzowl:

- 88% of video marketers report that video gives them a positive ROI. By comparison, only 33% felt that way 5 years ago.
- 97% of marketers say video has helped increase user understanding of their product or service.
- 76% say it helped them increase sales.
- 47% say it helped them reduce support queries.
- 76% say it helped them increase traffic.
- 80% say video has increased dwell time on their website (aka how long a person stays on the site).

And if those statistics aren't enough to convince you that video is the most powerful medium out there, here are some more that should. According to HubSpot, 7 out of 10 B2B buyers watch a video at some point in the sales or buying process. With B2C, it's even higher. 95% of people have watched an explainer video to learn more about a product or service, and 84% have been convinced to buy a product or service by watching a brand's video.

7 out of 10! 95%! 84%! These are huge numbers, and you should take them seriously. If you want to win the marketing battle, you need to pay attention. Video isn't just the way of the future. It's the marketing *present*.

If you're not already using video, you're fighting an uphill battle.

These statistics show that video should be a no-brainer, but here's the deal. The majority of businesses still aren't leading their branding stories with video. Almost every company I come into contact with is grossly deficient when it comes to utilizing video to grow their bottom line and to create a great brand.

And do you know what? They're missing a *major* opportunity. Video is one of the best ways to tell your story, make authentic connections, and build lasting connections with customers. You may not be able to go door-to-door in your entire sales territory and form a personal relationship with everyone you meet, but you *can* convey something original, genuine, and fresh about yourself through compelling video. Customers learn through stories and metaphors.

Stop and think about it for a second. When your sales team goes on a call, do they hand the client a picture and script, or do they interact with the client and form a real, personal connection?

Duh. It would be *bizarre*, not to mention off-putting, if someone just showed up at your business and handed you reading material without ever saying a word. But that's exactly what you're doing when you decide not to use video. You're leaving your customer to ignore you or fill in all the personality gaps.

Don't tell your story that way—or at least not *only* that way. Use video to tell your brand story through living, breathing, charismatic human beings. Connection is always more effective.

YOUR BRAND IS YOUR REPUTATION

All in all, Marco Rubio's presidential bid didn't go so well. He lost the Republican primary elections in 49 states, and finished 4th overall nationally. But for the one state my firm was called in to assist—Minnesota—we stuck to the 5 steps of the Undefeated Marketing System and saw obvious results.

Marco Rubio's "reset" ad clearly struck a chord with Minnesota voters. Using video, he delivered the message they wanted to hear, and he sustained that authentic message over the course of his whole campaign. That's one of the reasons why Marco Rubio swept the Minnesota primary with such a large margin.

Here's something every political marketer knows—and that every corporate marketer should take into account. Your brand isn't about your slogan, logo, or ad campaign. It's about the give-and-take relationship you have with customers. Your brand should evoke an emotional connection with your customers. Otherwise, you're wasting your money.

In today's day and age, there's rarely just one thing that converts a customer immediately. It usually takes several pieces of the pizza pie, and it also takes time. Your brand is your reputation. It had better be consistent—across every tasty slice—and it better be real.

Once you've moved through Step 3 and developed a data-backed, strategic, emotional brand, you've gone a long way toward eliminating your marketing campaign's risk. But you're not out of the woods yet.

If your brand is your reputation, you want to make sure that it's going to resonate with your customers and clients. And I don't mean just an "Oh, that's nice" kind of resonate. I mean *blow them out of the water*.

Content creation isn't always an exact science, no matter how much data is behind it. That's what makes the next step, testing, so important.

CHAPTER 5

STEP 4: TEST YOUR DATA-BACKED MESSAGING TO PROVE WHAT WILL WORK

POLITICS IN AMERICA HAS NEVER BEEN MORE POLARIZED. But no matter what side of the political spectrum you fall on, we can probably all agree on one thing: Donald Trump's campaigns were astoundingly successful when it came to online marketing.

As the director of digital marketing and fundraising for Trump's 2016 campaign, Gary Coby was instrumental in making that success happen. According to the American Association of Political Consultants, Gary executed nearly $100 million in digital media and raised more than a quarter of a billion dollars online, in only 5 months.

Those numbers are staggering by any measure. And the 2016 election results were even more staggering. Donald Trump—the unlikeliest candidate in modern history—walked away with 304 electoral college votes, compared to Hillary Clinton's 227.

When I asked Gary, "What was the most effective thing you did during that campaign?" he shared the following insights.

By overlaying consumer data and voter data (Step 1), Gary and his team knew that Facebook was the digital platform showing the largest growth for votes. That's why they built their 2016 marketing strategy almost entirely around Facebook (Step 2).

Their research had also given them a deep understanding of what their target voters cared about—issues like immigration and national security—and what kind of messaging would resonate with voters. For example, they knew that Trump's dedication to building a border wall and his repeated emphasis on Hillary Clinton's use of a private email address and servers while she was Secretary of State would move their target voters to action. The Trump campaign built their entire brand (Step 3) around the information and strategy they gathered in the first 2 steps. His brand was "Make America Great Again."

That's all part of good political marketing, and it was crucial to the campaign's runaway success on social media. But here's where the really innovative part of Gary's vision came in: ad testing.

The Trump campaign used cheap Facebook banner ads to run a single message 163 different ways. I said that right. They made slight changes to every ad. And when I say "slight," I mean *slight*. They might have changed the hair color of the woman in the ad, the color of the background, or the fonts on the text.

Then, for the next few weeks, they collected data on which of those ads performed the best. Inevitably, 5 to 10 out of that whole sea of ads rose to the top. They didn't know why. They didn't know how. The message was the same for all 163 ads, but their testing proved some big winners.

It was almost amazing how consistent the results were, considering how minor the changes were. They found that those tiny differences had a huge impact on how many people engaged with the campaign.

By the time Gary's team poured the majority of their marketing money into a specific ad campaign, they had *reams* of data about what kinds of ads would resonate best with their target voters—down to the last detail.

They knew with 99.9% certainty which ads were going to catch a voter's attention (and which ones wouldn't work), and those were the kinds of ads they moved "full steam ahead" with (Step 5).

It was a genius tactic, and that's why it paid off so well. Who would have thought that measly banner ads could help sway an entire presidential election? But they did.

And the reason they did is because Gary and his team didn't think of the banner ads in terms of ROI. They thought of them as a *tool* that would show them how to make that return on investment even greater.

Look, these are variations on banner ads, and most of them aren't effective tools for conversion. Very few people click them. But they are much cheaper than video ads. That makes them a highly effective way to test a marketing campaign.

If a potential customer clicks on a banner ad, that means your message and your creative has really resonated with them. And once you know what hooks your customers and clients, you can confidently move forward knowing that your ads will work on a larger scale.

Here's the real beauty of the 5-step Undefeated Marketing System: each step gives you a chance to reduce your risk before you pour all your marketing dollars into an expensive ad campaign.

One of the most important steps for reducing your risk is Step 4, the testing phase. Before you launch, you have to test minor variations of creative and messaging to see what's going to click with customers. That way, when you move on to Step 5 (launch), you'll have an almost foolproof shot at marketing success.

WHY TESTING MATTERS

One of Western Canada's largest commercial construction companies reached out to me because they needed help converting high-value customers and driving high-value leads. Emphasis on "high-value" and "high-quality." This was a B2B company, and they weren't looking to bring in 100 customers a week. All they needed was to land 1 good contract.

Our Customer Insights Report told us everything we needed to know about this company's ideal client. Their high-value clients wanted trust, safety, and quality service—all of which aligned with our client's preexisting reputation.

But we also found a unique alignment that our client hadn't tapped into. Their ideal customers cared about being culturally and environmentally sensitive, and our client had strong partnerships and working agreements with First Nations (Canada's name for Indigenous peoples). They also gave employees training in aboriginal affairs and took community engagement seriously. Not to mention they also actively recruit, train, and mentor Indigenous workers.

Now, that's a significant difference. There weren't many other construction companies that could use that as a selling point—and more importantly, that was a selling point that mattered to their target clients.

We ran with it. We built our strategic marketing around those findings, and we created content designed to get the attention of those high-value contracts. Our test ads prompted, *Is your civil contractor First Nations?* and *Do you value Indigenous partnerships?* We focused not just on how our client was an industry leader—which they were—but also on how much they cared about Indigenous communities.

Then we moved on to Step 4. We started with a 3-month testing period, where we used digital banner ads and pre-roll video (the ads that play before a featured video). Why? Because, in the testing phase, it's a lot cheaper than investing in a full ad campaign, but it still gave us a chance to see how the ads resonated with their clients. We had clear optics, inexpensively.

And speaking of clients, during the testing phase, we targeted 6 specific high-value companies and their key decision-makers. This was a limited testing pool, but it would help us increase our client's brand awareness, and it gave us a great opportunity to see which ads would get the job done.

But here's the thing. We weren't just sending short videos and banner ads to 6 people and calling it a day. This testing phase was also critical to our larger strategy. We were able to use these tests to build a retargeting pool of high-quality leads. If you don't know what a retargeting pool is, don't worry. You learn more about them in Chapter 7.

For now, here's what you need to know: once a potential customer clicks on an ad, you can move them into a retargeting pool and keep sending ads their way. That's why, when you look at a pair of shoes on Amazon, the picture of the ad follows you around and keeps popping up on every website you visit. If this has happened to you before...congratulations! You've entered a retargeting pool.

So, basically, when someone clicked on this client's test ads, we knew that we had made headway. They were curious and wanted to discover more. They were prime candidates for the full-on marketing campaign (Step 5).

Once we knew which ads were most successful, we doubled down and ran a high-volume mix of them to our retargeting pool of leaders from the initial 6 companies. These folks all had the power to review bids, interview companies, and award contracts. They were the big fish in the pond, and thanks to our testing phase, we already knew they were intrigued by the dangling bait.

In the end, that strategy ended up landing our client a massive, high-value contract with one of their targeted companies. And over the course of their 6-month campaign, their ads had been viewed 2 million times, which resulted in high-value website visitors from our target audience. In other words, they caught the big fish they wanted, and they had plenty more ready to bite.

I can't overstate how important that testing phase was to getting our client the results they wanted. Here's why.

Our client knew that banner ads weren't an effective way to convert business. Rarely is there a "sale" there. But they still trusted us that our cheap banner ads were an effective way to figure out what would work best, at a low cost.

Come on, how often do you really click on a banner ad to make a purchase of a product or service? Be honest.

Right. Never. (Or pretty close.) So, if someone *does* click through on a still photo, banner ad, or motion graphic, that's telling you something important. That tells you that your ad is working.

The testing phase gave us the chance to refine our messaging and our creative to make sure it was generating enough curiosity to make viewers click to learn more about the company we represented—something they wouldn't normally do.

It also gave us the chance to put our client's name (brand) at the forefront of their potential customers' brains. Even if the target audience didn't click through on the banner or pre-roll ads, they were still seeing our client's name everywhere before the contract decisions were made.

Then, when we launched the full ad campaign, they already had a sense of who our client was. They were much more likely to watch our client's content, simply because they recognized their name. Never underestimate the power of brand recognition.

Here's something important to remember. Customers rarely buy something the first time they see it. They need to have your brand or product's name drilled into their head before it registers. If marketing is a battle for a customer's attention, think of testing as the advance guard of soldiers that shows up beforehand to assess the situation. Those tests lead the way and make preparations so when the full army shows up, they'll be 100% ready to conquer.

The testing phase has one final benefit too. It helps you zero in on your target customer or client. In this case, we started with a pretty narrow field—6 companies—but really, we were gunning for *one* contract. Some e-commerce companies we run campaigns for aim for hundreds, thousands, or millions of customers. It doesn't matter how big your audience is, *testing before you spend big on your marketing will ensure you refine your target and have more success.*

From our initial testing pool of 6 companies, we started to see patterns. We learned which decision-makers in certain geographic locations were most interested in our client's test ads, and that gave us a better picture of who was most likely to convert down the line. By the time we launched (Step 5), we had a crystal-clear idea of which leaders, specifically, we should be targeting.

This is the perfect example of why testing matters. Testing isn't about growing your bottom line. It's about learning what *will* grow your bottom line.

Testing is about getting an *even better* handle on your customer or client, creative, and message. It's about reducing your risk as much as possible before you spend most of your marketing dollars. Then, when you're ready to launch, you can invest with reasonable certainty about what's going to break through the advertising clutter and drive maximum conversions.

ARE YOUR ADS BREAKING THROUGH THE CLUTTER?

We were working with a regional furniture chain who had been running the same kinds of ads for *years*. For their annual Labor Day sale, they printed up an 8-page brochure to mail to potential customers. You read that right: *8 pages*.

It was an antiquated advertising method, and as you can probably imagine, it ate up a huge portion of their annual advertising budget. We suspected that it wasn't our client's best way to spend their ad dollars, but we couldn't be certain because this client didn't even have a metric in place to see how the campaign had affected their sales every year.

We didn't want to ditch this traditional tactic if it was actually working. We didn't know, but we suspected they could improve their ROI. In some cases, old-school mail works better than you may think. According to Compu-Mail, up to 90% of direct mail gets opened (compared to only 20% to 30% of emails).

In this particular client's case, our Customer Insights Report (Step 1) told us that direct mail resonated well with their particular customer base. But we also learned that a majority of that audience spends 20-plus hours online every week.

Our strategic marketing plan (Step 2) focused on leveraging *both* of those data points. We came up with a plan to mail a (much cheaper) 1-page (2-sided) big, glossy postcard with a tantalizing offer. Then we would deliver the same creative in social media ads to the exact same target customer on their mailing list. (This tactic is known as a "digital mail chase.") That way, we'd have 2 bites of the apple. They'd see our client's ad in their mailboxes, and they'd see it again while they surfed Instagram.

I always believe that in order for direct mail to work, it needs to evoke emotion that triggers a response or allows people to imagine—how will acting on this offer make my life better? So, during Step 3, we used attractive furniture images to evoke a modern yet comfortable look. It felt appealing but attainable. Based on what our customer data said, we included a strong call to action that offered a sizable discount.

Now, up to this point, all of our data had pointed to the same thing: this strategy was going to work better than the traditional and expensive 8-page mailer, and it was going to cost a hell of a lot less. But before we ditched a method that this client had been using for years, we needed to be sure. We needed to see what was more effective: running ads the same way they'd always done or trying a new, updated method. In other words, we needed to test it (Step 4).

We identified a small number of "high-intent" potential customers who were likely to act based on receiving a piece of direct mail. Then we broke them into 2 subsets. Group A received the historically used 8-page mailer, while Group B received the newly designed mailer *plus* follow-up digital chase ads pushing them to check out the Labor Day sale.

So what happened? By the time we launched (Step 5), we knew—without a doubt—that our new method would be far more effective on customers (and cost-effective for our client) than the antiquated 8-page brochure. And the results were staggering. The direct mail plus digital chase campaign brought in $1,882,790 in revenue, and the number of people who clicked through on their digital ads was 4 times higher than the industry average. Our client spent *less* money and saw a 23× ROI. Let's say that again: *a 23× ROI.*

Do you want those kinds of results? *Then don't skip Step 4, and invest money in tests to find out what works best before launching (Step 5).*

I could talk until I'm blue in the face about why testing is great, but at the end of the day, it really boils down to 1 thing: testing helps you understand which ads will cut through the clutter.

I'm reminded of a quote by the economist Herbert Simon: "A wealth of information leads to a poverty of attention." There's too much competition for attention right now. So, before you spend boatloads of money on an 8-page brochure (or whatever other advertising method you've been using for years), make sure you test various messages and platforms to ensure your highest ROI possible when you launch your marketing campaign.

The only way to know whether your messaging and ad placement will cut through the clutter—without breaking the bank, of course—is to test it with low-budget ads. You'll know in a matter of weeks, and sometimes a matter of days, what will work on a larger scale (and what won't).

HOW CAN YOU CREATE A SUCCESSFUL TEST CAMPAIGN?

I need to make something clear. When you're testing ads, you run a wide variety of ads. You might test different products, different platforms, slightly different messaging, a positive ad and a negative ad, and so on. When you do that, you're not just testing things willy-nilly, hoping that 1 of those messages will work.

Based on the data, strategy, and branding, you already know that *all* of those ads will work. You just don't know which combination of message, product, and platform will get the highest returns.

Testing isn't about throwing everything into the marketplace and seeing what sticks. It's about throwing the *right* data-backed messaging into the *right* data-backed marketplace and seeing which ad blows every other good ad out of the water.

There will almost always be a clear winner (or winners) when you test. For example, one of our apparel clients hired us to come up with a special Black Friday marketing campaign (which we launched 3 weeks before Black Friday). After working through their customer data (Step 1), strategy (Step 2), and brand (Step 3), we ran 6 different test ads targeting women. Right away, one rose to the top. An ad focusing on "that cozy Christmas-morning feeling" showed a relaxed woman in comfortable clothes, lounging on the sofa with her significant other. It outperformed all the other ads with women aged 18 to 34.

Another data-backed ad showed a model holding up a pair of pants, and it said, "Thanksgiving Pants. You'll be thankful for them." That ad performed the worst. Moving forward, guess which one we went with?

Our customer data had told us that these customers liked to shop on the holidays and they loved "deals." But who knew that they were more apt to buy our client's clothes with a Christmas ad than with a Thanksgiving ad? Testing the message gave us the proof we needed before we spent our client's marketing budget on a huge ad campaign.

That's a crucial point. In today's day and age, you can't run a one-size-fits-all strategy. There's no way you're going to run one ad and have it appeal to both 18-year-olds and 82-year-olds. Consumers just don't work that way.

So, really, when you're testing your ads, you're also testing your target customer. Depending on what your customer data from Step 1 tells you, you'll be running a lot of different ads to different audiences to see which ones drive the most conversions.

Look, you can find the biggest diamond in the world, but until you polish it up and make it shine, all most people are going to see is a big hunk of dirty rock. Steps 1 through 3 are all about finding and digging out that precious gem, but unless you spend your time in Step 4 refining it, you're not going to be ready to dazzle the world.

Testing is all about fine-tuning the message, audience, content, and platform that will drive the best ROI. That's where you should put all your energy before you spend big bucks. Don't cut corners when the end is so near.

TESTING ISN'T NEW, BUT MOST MARKETERS AREN'T DOING IT RIGHT

Your corporate marketing agency will probably tell you, "We *do* run tests," and it's true. They do. But most of the time they run tests that cost an arm and a leg because they don't want to prove their ads before spending your money. After all, if they can take a big piece of the financial pie during the testing phase and *another* piece of the pie during the actual campaign, they've just made themselves a pretty hefty profit.

I can't tell you how many business owners have told me, "My marketing agency definitely tested, but they made me spend $100,000, which is a lot of money for us. Then, once the agency went out and ran the tests, they came back and said, 'All right, let's go spend $250,000 now that we know what works.'"

Excuse me? They just set you back $100,000? And now they want you to spend another quarter of a million? That's great for the marketing agency, but I don't have to tell you how terrible it is for you, their client.

In *Fire Them Now*, I revealed one of corporate marketers' most prevalent lies: you have to spend big to discover what works. That makes absolutely no sense. Why would you invest big money on a marketing campaign before you know what will resonate with your customers?

You don't need to spend tons of money on a bunch of cookie-cutter concepts and pray that one pays off.

Trust me. Political marketers have made an art out of taking a tiny amount of money and squeezing every bit of value from it. And we do that by testing ads at a low budget to find out exactly what's going to hit voters hardest. Only after we prove what will work do we spend the biggest chunk of the client's ad budget. That's exactly what I did during one of the most competitive state senatorial campaigns in the country.

During a hotly contested election season, the Florida Republican Senatorial Campaign Committee asked my agency to come up with a strategy to help them keep Florida's upper chamber red.

Based on our Voter Insights Report (the political version of the Customer Insights Report) we knew that the race was going to hinge on our ability to win over undecided mom voters. More specifically, we needed to win over young women voters with young children in the household.

Our Voter Insights Report revealed that their children's most-watched TV show was *Bob the Builder*. (Yes, we knew down to the exact detail what their kids were watching and what these moms would recognize.)

In case you aren't as familiar with *Bob the Builder* as a parent of young children might be, the show is just what it sounds like. An animated building contractor named Bob works alongside his pals to finish construction projects, solve problems, and cooperate. The iconic theme tune starts with Bob's catchphrase, "Can we fix it?" to which the other characters enthusiastically chant, "Yes, we can!"

We knew that if we ran a *Bob the Builder*-themed ad to these moms, they would recognize it, and it would cut through the clutter of thousands of other ads competing for their attention. Not only that, they would probably laugh at it and engage with our message.

The stars aligned, and it just so happened that the Democratic candidate we needed to beat was named Bob. Seriously. It couldn't have been more perfect. So we got to work with a little building project of our own. We created an animated political ad called "Bob the Bilker."

As a cartoon Bob ran around town racking up exorbitant costs, moms heard that Bob the Bilker was "running up job costs on our children's school district." We used the same font, high-energy tone, and catchy theme music as the TV show. But instead of Bob's catchphrase, moms heard, "Will he cheat us?" and a refrain, "Yes, he will!"

Even though steps 1 through 3 told us that this kind of messaging was likely to resonate, we still needed to test it (Step 4). So we tested it by running the ad on digital platforms used by mothers with young children.

It tested through the roof. The return was like catching lightning in a bottle. It was so incredible, we immediately knew we had to run the ad on a much larger scale, and it had the potential to help us win the race. We launched it (Step 5), and for the final 3 weeks of the campaign, the ad ran in local TV markets.

Bob never recovered from the "Bilker" label, and he ended up losing in the most expensive state senate race in Florida history by 7%. The ad was so effective, it won several national awards, including "Best Ad for an Independent Expenditure Campaign."

The bottom line was that even before we went into the testing phase, we knew what was going to resonate with voters. But instead of jumping in whole hog, we used a small budget to test on strategic digital platforms that would give us a reliable sense of the ad's success.

We only launched it on a larger scale once the ad blew the roof off return numbers, and by that point, we knew that we wouldn't be wasting our precious advertising dollars.

Testing doesn't have to be expensive. In fact, it shouldn't be.

When your marketing agency tells you that every dollar you spend on advertising is the same and that it takes a fat check to execute a test campaign, *don't listen*. If you want to get the most bang for your buck, you have to start small with your testing budget, then test and refine several times before ever making a large marketing investment.

By testing your ads before you launch the full marketing campaign, you eliminate your risk. You put yourself in a position to succeed before you spend the majority of your budget.

Here's the difference between someone who's "committed" to their marketing success versus someone who's "interested." The "committed" business owner sees the 5 steps all the way through to the end, while the interested business owner wonders why the testing phase didn't convert a 10× return and then quits before they see all 5 steps to fruition.

STOP THROWING MONEY AT THE WRONG PROBLEMS

In 2016, the Trump campaign had a lot of money. They could have thrown a huge budget at online marketing from the get-go, eliminated the ads that didn't work, and still have had plenty of funds left over to run a great campaign.

But that's not what they did. They knew there was no point in wasting money on ads that weren't going to work. Instead, they stuck to small-scale tests, spent less money, and actually had a better gauge of what was going to work for their target voters when they were ready to launch Step 5.

Low-budget ads are often a better indicator of your message and creative power because there are no bells and whistles to pull a customer in. If the message and creative works at its most basic, it will work once you bring it to life on a larger, fuller scale.

That's the power of testing. Once you have a message and content that you know works, you can launch your marketing campaign virtually risk-free.

CHAPTER 6

STEP 5: LAUNCH YOUR DATA-BACKED MARKETING CAMPAIGN

IN 2016, I SPENT A LOT OF TIME THINKING ABOUT 3 STATES: Florida, New Hampshire, and North Carolina. Those 3 states are always battleground states during presidential elections.

When I was hired by a super PAC to work on behalf of Donald Trump's 2016 presidential campaign, I immediately knew that Florida, New Hampshire, and North Carolina were crucial to win. We set our sights on persuadable undecided voters in those 3 states, hoping to swing them to the win column.

We followed the 5-step Undefeated Marketing System to a T. We gathered data about those persuadable undecided voters (Step 1). Most of them were "sliders," or voters who were liable to shift their votes in the last few weeks of the campaign.

We needed those voters because the Trump campaign already

had a solid idea of how dyed-in-the-wool Republican voters were going to turn out. We also knew that we weren't likely to convince dyed-in-the-wool Democrats to change sides. They hated Trump, and they weren't budging. If we wanted to turn the tide of the election in these 3 swing states, we had to focus on these swing voters—the ones with open minds who were ready to be persuaded.

After we had an ocean-deep understanding of who those "sliders" were and what they cared about, we used it to put together a strategic marketing plan on how to target them and put them in the Trump basket of voters (Step 2). Then we created videos that we knew, based on our voter data, would hit all the points these target voters cared about and wanted to see and hear (Step 3).

Marketers know that they've struck gold when someone watches their 30- to 60-second video ad all the way to the end. Stop and ask yourself this question: Are you going to watch a video advertisement that's as dull as dishwater all the way to the end?

No way. No one watches a full 30- to 60-second ad unless it grabs them.

So, when voters (or customers or clients) would rather watch the rest of your ad than jump ahead to the video they *want* to see, you know your ad isn't just working. It's a home run.

When the fate of a presidential election is on the line, you don't want to bore people. You want to knock their socks off. You want to inspire them. You want to create something so powerful, they can't take their eyes off it.

That's why you test (Step 4). You need to know that your data-backed branded content isn't just going to resonate with voters—because Step 1 already assures that it will. You need to know that it's going to resonate in the most powerful, earth-shaking, emotionally gut-wrenching way possible.

You want an ad that's going to have a completion rate that's off the charts. A completion rate is exactly what it sounds like: the percentage of people who watch your ad all the way to the end. If you've got a high completion rate, you know you've successfully captured your audience's attention. You know you've got the right ad and it will lead to votes or conversions.

By the time we launched our full-scale campaign (Step 5) for the Trump super PAC, we were confident from our testing that our content was going to grab the right voters by the arm and guide them all the way to the voting booth.

For this particular ad, we targeted 6,333,864 voters in the 3 states that we deemed as "persuadable." When we launched the ad campaign, of those 6 million–plus voters, 4,653,705 watched the ad to completion. That gave us a completion rate of 73.47%, meaning almost 3-quarters of these persuadable voters who saw our ad watched it all the way through.

Look, that's *really* high. It was compelling enough that they weren't tempted to hit that "skip" button. It was powerful enough that these voters hung on our every word for the full 30 seconds. It was potent.

We weren't just reaching our target voters; we were flagging them down with flares and a giant neon SOS. We had their attention, which means that we were much more likely to sway their vote.

By the time election night rolled around, we saw the fruits of our labors. Out of those 3 battleground states, North Carolina and Florida were clear victories. In New Hampshire, Trump lost—but only by 2,736 votes.

Here's the truth. No marketing is perfect; you're not going to win everything. No matter how directly your content speaks to your target audience, you're not going to corner 100% of the market and inspire loyalty in every single customer.

Not even mega-companies like Apple and Google can pull that off. They do a great job; don't get me wrong. But there's no such thing as perfection.

What you *can* aim for is a consistent series of home runs. You can hit the ball over the fences and edge out the competition, 1 swing at a time.

Did our ad help bring Trump a flawless victory in all 3 states? No. But it did help secure victory in a couple of key states that decided the election, and it brought us a hell of a lot closer in New Hampshire, which is a trending blue state.

In fact, let's put this into perspective. In 2012, Barack Obama beat Mitt Romney by 39,643 votes in New Hampshire.

Now compare that margin to the 2,736 votes Hillary Clinton eked out for her win. Trump may have lost in New Hampshire in 2016, but his campaign made huge gains.

Because we followed the Undefeated Marketing System, we were reasonably certain that we would win over the persuadable voters we needed in those critical states. There's always some chance involved when it comes to the actual voter turnout, but we weren't firing shots in the dark.

We knew that we had delivered the right content to the right voters in the right way. That meant that by the time Election Day rolled around, we were as close to certain as we humanly could be.

That's the real beauty of the 5-step system; by the time you launch your marketing campaign (Step 5), you've mitigated almost all of your risk. There's little guesswork or gambling involved. You're looking at verifiable growth.

THE POWER OF A SUCCESSFUL STEP 5 LAUNCH

How do you think moms respond when their kids' options for success are threatened?

I can tell you, I don't want to be on the receiving end of that kind of fury. But that's exactly where one of the most anti-education-reform governors in the nation, Louisiana governor John Bel Edwards, found himself.

To give you some context, the previous governor, Bobby Jindal, had made it his mission to improve educational opportunities for low-income and mostly minority kids across the state of Louisiana. (By the way, I was Bobby Jindal's campaign manager during his run for governor.) He saw that massive amounts of kids were stuck in failing, dangerous public schools, with no way out. We knew those kids needed better options.

I worked with an organization called the American Federation for Children to create a marketing campaign that helped pass the first-ever school choice bill. "School choice" gave parents the option of pulling their children out of those unsafe and failing public schools and putting them into a better school of their choice—whether that was a private school, a charter school, or another public school. Thousands of low-income, mostly minority children were given scholarships to support the cost of tuition through a program called the Louisiana Scholarship Program.

For possibly the first time in their lives, these kids had a real shot at a better education and a brighter future. But when Governor John Bel Edwards came into office, he had made it his mission to destroy the Louisiana Scholarship Program. He wanted to eliminate the program entirely, but he knew he didn't have the votes to do it. So, instead, he planned to cut the program by millions and millions of dollars.

You'd better believe the American Federation for Children wasn't going to take that lying down. They hired us to come in and run a marketing campaign to stop him.

We needed to exert pressure on Governor Edwards and raise such a fuss that he couldn't move ahead with his plans. To do that, we needed to create public awareness about his proposed cuts, show just how harmful the cuts would be to these deserving families, and stir up a passionate response from his constituents. Basically, we needed to create enough noise to stop him in his tracks.

When we analyzed our target audience data (Step 1), we found that authentic parent voices (not actors) were going to be the most effective communicators to save the scholarship program. Hearing directly from the parents and students involved would be the surest way to tug at people's heartstrings and move them to take action against Edwards's proposed cuts. We needed to get them so riled up that they would reach out to their legislators, as well as Governor Edwards's office, to demand full funding for the program.

Next, we asked ourselves, "What is the message, and where do we need to take it?" and developed a strategic plan (Step 2) around the answers. A huge proportion of the affected students lived in metropolitan areas like Baton Rouge and New Orleans, so we planned to target those regions with our campaign. We wanted people to see just how devastating Edwards's budget cuts would be to their communities.

We also knew we needed to create a message that would make the governor's jaw drop to the ground. We wanted him to know, as soon as he saw it, that he was going to be in a world of trouble. So we decided to go to a school in Baton Rouge where a lot of Louisiana Scholarship Program kids were safe, happy, and thriving. We planned to level with their parents and tell them, flat out, "John Bel Edwards plans to take your kid out of this unbelievable private school and put them back in the failing public school they were in before." We knew that would give us the authentic, emotional, and compelling response we needed to motivate our target audience.

We weren't wrong. The parents and kids felt betrayed. They were devastated for their kids. And they were prepared to help us fight back. We worked with a group of African American moms to create a brand (Step 3) called "John Bel Failed Us." We created a website, petitions, stories, and ads. In one particularly powerful ad, the moms stare straight at the camera, their voices quaking with emotion and rage, and say, "John Bel Edwards broke his word. He lied. He lied to me. He lied to my child. He turned his back on us."

Then the ad reveals their heartbroken kids, struck with the news that they're going to have to leave the schools they love. One boy clutches his backpack sadly in a hallway. One girl looks longingly at the playground she'll miss. One girl wears her private-school uniform in front of an empty classroom. Finally, the ad cuts back to the faces of the disillusioned moms, giving viewers one last glimpse of the disappointment and resentment bubbling just below the surface.

The end of the ad told viewers, "Get the facts. Add your voice. Visit JohnBelFailedUs.com." When they visited that branded site, they had the chance to learn even more about the cause—and how they could join the grassroots movement against Edwards's proposed cuts.

Yes, the ad was vicious. But do you know what? It was also *honest*. It was authentic, and that's what made it so powerful. We weren't going for the jugular for no reason. The governor had threatened the future of these families, and these parents were prepared to defend their kids' schools. Anyone who watched our ad could immediately sympathize with the anger and grief of those mothers.

We tested the ad (Step 4) in one of our target markets, and it blew up. The ad was so emotional and authentic, it brought a lot of viewers to tears. We knew, beyond a shadow of a doubt, that this campaign was going to get us the public attention and the Edwards jaw-drop that we needed.

When we launched (Step 5), we ran this campaign on digital platforms, TV, radio, and mailers in our target market. We even ran a telemarketing campaign (yes, it was legal) where we had volunteers directly call parents and inform them about what the governor was planning to do. We struck so hard and fast, Governor Edwards never knew what hit him.

The video ad went viral, reaching almost 2 million people. The campaign also garnered more than 30 articles in local and national news outlets like US News and World Report and the *Washington Times*. If Governor Edwards had failed to listen to these moms before, he sure as hell had to pay attention now.

This ad struck such a deep, emotional chord with its audience that legislators at the state and national level were flooded with more than 20,000 phone calls from irate voters demanding action.

Governor Edwards held a press conference to try to defend himself, but it didn't work. These parents—and their advocates—weren't going to roll over. They wanted accountability, and they didn't want a dime to be taken from the Louisiana Scholarship Program.

What was the end result? Not only did the Louisiana Scholarship Program survive. It was actually *expanded*. Our campaign secured an additional $4 million to give low-income children a chance at a better education.

The "John Bel Failed Us" campaign ended up being the most successful marketing campaign I've executed in my career. I say that not only because of the remarkable press coverage and the incredible traction the campaign received. I also say that because that campaign *helped low-income families in need*. Think of all the lives that money has changed. All those moms got to keep their kids in high-performing schools they had chosen. All those children had a chance to thrive and break out of poverty. And all those politicians, Governor Edwards included, learned just how important school choice was to voters.

The "John Bel Failed Us" campaign gave us results beyond our wildest dreams. Actually, no. I can't say they were beyond our wildest dreams because we *knew exactly what we were aiming for*. We wanted a safe and secure future for those low-income children. And we refused to settle for less.

Isn't it time you did the same with your business marketing? Why settle for marketing campaigns that give you less than your wildest dreams? Why don't you set your sights on the most powerful launch you can imagine and use the 5 steps to make those dreams reality?

Maybe it's time to stop selling your company short.

When you launch a marketing campaign, you aren't just sticking an ad here and a video there. You're not just slapping some copy up on your website and hoping it works. You're not focusing on what you think is a catchy slogan and perfect logo. A successful marketing launch is much more than the sum of its parts.

You're building a fortress, brick by brick. That fortress is so incredible—so compelling and masterfully built—that every customer will want to see it. They won't be able to stay away. And the best part? Because your fortress is built on the foundation of empathy, strategy, and data-tested content, that sucker will be *strong*, and you'll be protected from almost all possible risk.

You can also think about a successful marketing campaign as a strategic chess game, where "checkmate" means you've delivered on all your customers' deepest needs and values. Every move matters, and if you skip a step or make a mistake, it might cost you the game.

Unless you've got some powerful marketing karma on your side, there's no way you can achieve that kind of long-term, sustainable precision with a wild game of trial-and-error. And even if you do get lucky, you probably won't replicate it. Lightning rarely strikes twice.

When it comes to launching an earth-shattering, wildly successful marketing campaign, luck won't cut it. If you want to be undefeated, you need a formula that's proven to work.

WHAT IS THE LIFETIME VALUE OF YOUR CUSTOMER/ CLIENT AND WHAT DO YOU WANT IT TO BE?

One of our clients came to us with a budget of $100,000 for a particular ad campaign.

They were on a tight deadline, and they were trying to enter a highly competitive market. We knew this was going to be anything but a piece of cake. But we had worked with this client before, and we were eager to help them out.

Before jumping in, we asked them about their goals. Our jaws dropped when they declared, "We want to make $500,000 from our $100,000 investment."

"Okay..." I hesitantly replied. "How did you get that number?"

"We made it up."

Well, I'll give them this—at least they were honest.

But let me put it gently. Your goals should not be a shot in the dark. If your answer to *anything* related to your marketing is "We made it up," it's time to sit down and have a long, hard think.

You need to go into this process knowing what you want and why you want it. If you don't have a clear, achievable goal, it doesn't matter how straight your arrow is or how good a marksman you are. You'll never hit an invisible target.

This happens to a lot of business owners, and I suffer from this sometimes as well. For example, last year, I stated I wanted to

15× my company. We had 9.6×-ed the company the year before, and 15 seemed like a good goal to me. But I had no real plans to make it happen.

Finally, my COO sat me down and said, "It's great that you want us to grow 15×, but what does that mean?" And it dawned on me that she was right.

Together, we sat down and made a multiyear plan to 3× in the first year, then 8× the following year. We wrote out all the steps that we would need to take to get there, like hiring people for business development, finding higher-paying clients, cutting down on certain kinds of expenses, and so on. All of a sudden, there was a real plan in place.

To take your business to the next level, you can't just shout "I want to grow 15×" and expect it to happen. You have to have a real plan with clear, achievable goals.

This would have been good advice for my client, but unfortunately, they weren't quite ready to move on from their arbitrary goal. They stuck to their guns with the made-up $500,000 number, and we resolved to get them the best results possible within their budget and time frame. We recalculated their goals and gave them a more realistic outcome, but they were still "hoping" for a $500,000 windfall.

We completed a full data analysis for them and came up with a competitive strategy involving retargeting pools (more on that in the next chapter). We created data-backed content, tested the ads, and launched, right on time.

From our perspective, the campaign went exceptionally well. The conversion rate and total sales exceeded our realistic projections, and they had a positive ROI. But our client wasn't happy, because the results didn't live up to their arbitrary $500,000 goal. Instead, they netted $140,076 in profit for a $100,000 ad spend.

I get it. If you're hoping to pull a rabbit out of a hat, you'll be disappointed if you get a dove. But guess what? You'll also miss the big picture—*magic still happened*.

Our client definitely wasn't looking at the big picture. If they had taken a deeper look at their results, they would have seen some important numbers that blew that $140,076 profit out of the water.

After the launch, their average customer spent *twice* as much as previous customers had, and they also showed a higher rate of returning customers. Those were quality customers. And if our client played their cards right, those customers were well on their way to being raving fans, or diehard, loyal brand advocates who live to spread the word about their favorite businesses.

Our client was so fixated on a short-term magic number that they had forgotten about the *lifetime value* of their customers. With this one ad campaign, we had changed the lifetime value of their customers from $66 to $91.

Look, it's easy to have a blowout sale and make a lot of money. It's harder to create a base of loyal customers who keep coming back for more. Every sign indicated that these customers would have been repeat purchasers. Even if the immediate return was lower than our client's randomly selected number, the long-term results would speak for themselves.

I point this out because it's one I see over and over. I'll work with clients to come up with a data-driven strategy that gets them gains, but then they're disappointed with the results. Why? Not because the results aren't there. But because *they haven't set achievable, data-driven goals.*

One of our other clients, who's in the e-commerce food space, took this to heart. When she first came to us, she was hesitant. She didn't want to run a competitive marketing campaign that broke even on the first sale (an average of $61). But once we sat down and explained the ways this would contribute to the *lifetime value* of her customers, she gave it a shot.

And, as we projected, they ended up having huge returns. Now, this e-commerce food company is up to an average customer lifetime value of $237, and they're not showing any signs of stopping. Let's put those numbers into perspective. The previous lifetime value of 1,000 customers totaled $61,000 in sales, but now, that same 1,000 customers will make the company $237,000. That's the power of loyalty.

This client listened when we told them that their initial gains were just that—initial. If you want to really understand the gains your company makes, you need clear, achievable goals, and more importantly, you need foresight. You must play the long game.

THE COMPOUND EFFECT

When you're in the early stages of the 5-step system, it may be easy to get discouraged by the relatively slow growth of your investment, but don't give in to your desire for instant gratification.

Why? Because the Undefeated Marketing System isn't the get-rich-quick scheme most marketers are selling these days. It's the most efficient and reliable way to tap into the compound effect.

If you're a business owner, you're probably familiar with compound interest. But, surprisingly, many business owners don't think about how powerful that same compound effect can be when it comes to their marketing gains.

Thanks to the compound effect, so-called small gains aren't always what they seem. Here's a great example, which comes from the renowned business strategist Tony Robbins. It's stuck with me ever since I heard it.

What if I said to you, "Let's go play a game of golf, and to make it a little more interesting, let's bet a dime a hole"?

Most people would say, "Sure!" There are only 18 holes. It doesn't seem like a lot of risk. $1.80 isn't a big deal.

But what if I decided to shake things up when we got to the first hole? What if I said, "Let's make this a little more interesting. Why don't we just double the bet at each hole?" So, the first hole is 10 cents; the second hole is 20 cents.

At first glance, that bet seems harmless too. But when you follow it all the way down the line, something surprising happens. Watch.

Third hole: $0.40
Fourth hole: $0.80
Fifth hole: $1.60
Sixth hole: $3.20
Seventh hole: $6.40
Eighth hole: $12.80
Ninth hole: $25.60
Tenth hole: $51.20
Eleventh hole: $102.40
Twelfth hole: $204.80
Thirteenth hole: $409.60
Fourteenth hole: $819.20
Fifteenth hole: $1,638.40
Sixteenth hole: $3,276.80
Seventeenth hole: $6,553.60
Eighteenth hole: $13,107.20

What started as a seemingly tiny, meaningless bet adds up quickly, thanks to compound growth. Before you know it, you're up to $13,000 in bets. If you're a good golfer, you might want to try this tactic next time you're playing an inferior partner. It's quite the payoff.

The Undefeated Marketing System works the same way. During the first few steps, you're making a small investment to gather data, come up with a strategy, develop your brand, and run some tests. But before you know it, you're up to Step 5, and you're ready to launch (which is like walking up to the 6th hole). Because you've put in the work on the first few "holes," your growth will skyrocket faster than you expected.

Don't believe me? Here's a great example of the compound effect in action. One of my most successful clients runs a law firm in New York. Before he started working with us, his firm had a minimal online presence, and their revenue stream mostly came from small referrals.

Small referrals might sound like a good thing, but they actually aren't the best way for lawyers to earn money. Every time another law firm farmed out a small client to this firm, they received a 30% kickback on all the profits. Those kinds of added fees will really screw up your profit margins, and it was a huge strain on our client's bottom line.

Our client needed to become his own lead generator so the firm could stop paying those hefty referral fees and keep more profit in their bank account.

This client was a rare bird—and a dream to work with—because he literally came to us and said, "Tell us what we need to do, and we'll do it." More importantly, he meant it.

During Step 1, we used our exclusive data to get a better handle on this law firm's ideal client base. The Customer Insights Report revealed some surprising information about their online behaviors. For example, the firm's potential client base spent a significant amount of time on non-cable TV streaming sites like YouTube TV, Hulu, and Roku. And when I say "significant," I mean it. These folks spent more than 40 hours streaming each week!

We also learned that these potential clients cared about trust and being treated fairly. They weren't looking for a slick lawyer in an Armani suit flaunting million-dollar cases. They wanted someone who made them feel at ease and whom they could trust to stand up for them, no matter what.

Our Customer Insights Report also indicated that the higher we could raise the firm's brand recognition, the more leads they'd generate. New York City is a crowded market for law firms, and our client needed to stand out from the crowd. We learned that nothing made an attorney more memorable to this target market than a memorable slogan. And once the slogan "hooked" these potential leads, third-party validation went a long way toward turning them into trusted clients.

Look, bottom line, these target customers wanted to win their cases. You don't hire a lawyer unless you think they can get you a W. But beyond that, these clients also cared about *how their law firm made them feel about winning.* If they needed an attorney, they wanted to hire a law firm that believed in their case. They wanted to feel like they could trust their attorney to deal with them fairly—and to fight for that win! Our Step 1 data showed that that's the "difference that would make the difference" to these clients.

We used that wealth of information to develop a data-backed strategic marketing plan (Step 2). We suggested that the firm needed to totally revamp their digital presence if they wanted to meet clients where they spent the majority of their time: online.

Once everyone was on board with the plan, we built a data-backed branding campaign (Step 3) that resonated with potential clients' most significant motivator: trust. Every element of our messaging emphasized the firm's dedication and assured potential clients that working (and winning) with this firm would give them peace of mind. We firmly positioned the firm's third-party 5-star reviews on the website so they were the first thing a potential client would see, immediately cultivating trust. The website, testimonial page, landing pages—every single aspect of the rebrand—reinforced the core message: *we care, and we have your back.*

We also created a video advertisement that hit all the points we knew would resonate with potential clients, and we made the founding attorney the face of the messaging. We branded the campaign around the memorable phrase "Better Call Paul," a riff on the TV show *Better Call Saul.*

Then we moved to Step 4 and applied a small advertising budget to test our client's messaging. For example, we ran test ad campaigns that educated clients about issues that could affect their families, including New York's child abuse case statute of limitations and workers' rights. Both campaigns tested through the roof.

Remember, you have to put in the work before you see results. But trust me, patience pays every time. By the time we got to this client's launch phase, we had a laser-focused, data-backed marketing campaign that we knew would drive growth for his firm. Step 5 is when you start seeing a real return on your investment.

When we launched (Step 5), the campaign resulted in a huge influx of new clients. Almost immediately, the firm was able to generate a huge amount of non-referral profit (their stated goal).

That was just the beginning, because pretty soon, the compound effect set in. Just take a look at some of our clients' other returns:

- Since the start of our partnership, the firm's website had experienced a 300% increase of new, unique visitors.
- The firm saw an 8× increase in new, non-referral clients per month, and 100% of those profits stayed within the firm.
- They experienced a month-over-month increase in new leads and clients across multiple practice areas.
- They significantly undercut the industry average for advertising. The client spent $3.07 per click on our ads, compared to an industry average of $85.29. You read that right. "Better Call Paul" was a hit.
- After seeing the ads, our client became the lead referral practice for a national, top-100 law firm that delegates cases throughout the country. My client wasn't looking for referral business, but he also managed to take his referral business to an unprecedented level. They loved it.

To put it bluntly, the campaign generated the largest growth the firm has ever seen, and the law firm's revenue is the highest it's ever been. Not to mention the firm is expanding at a shockingly fast rate. Within 6 months of working with us, the firm positioned itself to open a new office and expand its practice areas so it could adapt quickly.

This law firm emails us on an almost weekly basis saying, "You guys will never believe who contacted me this week..." Business is coming in so fast, it's hard to keep up, but believe me, the CEO of this law firm is unstoppable.

Why was this client's launch such a stellar success?

In a word, because he was *committed*. He trusted the 5-step process and committed to seeing it all the way through. He kept using the formula until he got that metaphorical eighteenth hole. *And he's still going!*

Don't you want to see these kinds of results? Don't you want to tap into the power of the compound effect?

Then make a commitment. Don't cut and run at the beginning of the steps, when it feels like you're only making 10 cents or 20 cents at a time.

WANT TO PUT YOUR UNDEFEATED MARKETING SYSTEM ON STEROIDS? HERE'S HOW

I'm a big believer that when you combine your PR efforts with the Undefeated Marketing System, you can put your marketing on steroids. You just have to know how to leverage your media coverage.

Here's what I mean by "leverage." When my book *Fire Them Now* was released, I made 2 appearances promoting it on the #1-rated morning cable news show in America, *Fox and Friends*. I also appeared on ESPN to promote the book. Those kinds of programs get millions of viewers every hour.

After making 3 national TV appearances, I had 4 new book sales. 4.

I wasn't discouraged, though, because I knew that wasn't the point. I knew that in today's environment, showing up on the *Today* show won't necessarily improve your sales.

Know what does? Leveraging those 3 national TV appearances to my target book-buying audience.

So we clipped my national TV appearances and used them as part of a pitch to get me on even more leverageable media that would help me sell books, like business and marketing podcasts—Gary Vaynerchuck, Adam Carolla, James Altucher, and Mike Dillard.

If you don't know Mike Dillard, he has a cultlike following and millions of downloads of his show. We used my previous PR as social proof to pitch Mike Dillard. Because I had Fox News, ESPN, and other TV appearances under my belt, he knew I would be a good on-air guest. He didn't have to take a shot on someone who was a bad fit for his loyal audience. And once I appeared on his podcast, I sold hundreds of copies of my book.

Since 2013, I've made over 350 national TV appearances, and I've leveraged every single one of them. I can honestly say that only 1% of people who've ever seen me on CNN, MSNBC, CBS, Fox News, Fox Business, or ESPN have seen the live broadcast. The other 99% of people have seen me on those networks when I promoted my appearances online.

Finding PR opportunities isn't enough. You have to promote those opportunities in ads, on social media, and wherever else your target audience will see them. Think of PR as another form of compound growth. It's one more dime that you can leverage so your pool of money keeps growing.

With our clients, we often partner with PR firms to enhance the publicity opportunities for our clients, and then we market the hell out of those PR opportunities to tap into the compound effect.

Here's how it worked for one of our clients, a state-based apparel company. Around the time of their marketing campaign launch (Step 5), we partnered with a PR company that booked our client 2 local news stories. A bunch of celebrities and athletes had been spotted wearing our client's gear, and those 2 programs wanted to interview the CEO about the company's growth.

Those 2 news opportunities were great. But just like my national TV appearances for *Fire Them Now*, they only reached a limited number of viewers when they aired live. If we wanted to truly capitalize on them, we knew we had to make them part of our existing marketing campaign.

For the next 2 weeks, we ran statewide ads featuring clips from those 2 appearances. Why? First, we knew that leveraging our client's PR this way would make it possible to reach a much bigger audience. Second, we knew we could *target* those ads to make sure that our client's ideal customers would see them. Third, we were able to *enhance the story we were already telling* in our client's advertising by showing customers that celebrities were using our client's products and that the CEO had caught the attention of reputable news sources.

By leveraging our client's PR, we were able to put our typical ad campaign on steroids and drive a lot of new traffic to their website. Immediately after the CEO's appearances, our client saw a peak of more than 6,000 website visits. That was nearly 5 times more than their usual traffic. And even after the peak tapered off, their baseline for daily site visits was still more than 2 times their pre-launch traffic. Just think about it. For a 2-week ad run, those are huge returns.

Want to know why PR works so well? Because it gives your business third-party validation, while a direct ad just tells customers how great your company's products or services are. If you're a customer, who are you more likely to believe—the person trying to make money off your purchase or the third party with no financial skin in the game? When you can get third-party validation of your product or service, it makes your product or service much more intriguing to consumers.

But remember—PR alone won't sell your product for you. If you really want to put your marketing on steroids, you have to *leverage* that PR and make sure your target customers/clients know just how much the media, influencers, celebrities, your current customers, or other third-party validators love your products or services too.

YOU HAVE TO ALWAYS KEEP ADAPTING

Your launch (Step 5) isn't just a one-time event. Launching requires you to continually optimize your marketing performance month after month, year after year.

As we've learned from major events like pandemics, social unrest, and unexpected economic turns, consumer sentiment changes constantly. Sometimes those changes take years, and sometimes they only take days. The companies that stay on top of those changes are the ones that are prepared to grow in any economic environment.

Here's a great example. As I mentioned in Chapter 2, Coca-Cola was one of the fastest companies to pivot during the coronavirus pandemic. At the end of 2019, they were running pleasure-focused ads with the slogan "Open a Coke, open happiness." Several months later—and almost overnight—they shifted millions of ad dollars to the coronavirus "safety" message "Staying apart is the best way to stay united."

Almost every time I've mentioned that in an interview, the interviewer laughs, like "Oh God, how ridiculous is Coke?" There's something cringe-worthy about how on-the-nose that message seems.

But you know what? The reality is that Coca-Cola isn't just a soda and beverage company. They're primarily a data company. They spend millions of dollars a day to know what their customers are thinking so they can market to them effectively. And when you see Coca-Cola shift their message in a matter of days, it's a tell. They don't change their message without a reason, and you can guarantee that their reason isn't "We made it up."

No matter how small or large your business is, you can learn from watching giant companies' marketing moves. Because I guarantee you, those companies are watching their customer preference data like hawks. Even if Coca-Cola's unity message makes you want to throw up, they're not going to run an ad like that unless their customer research told them to do it. That's sophisticated marketing in action.

Do you want your marketing to be sophisticated? Do you want to eliminate your risk? Then take a lesson from companies like Coca-Cola. It's not enough to just reach Step 5, clap your hands, and call it a day. You have to always keep adapting. That is what modern-day marketing is all about.

Of course, you're not reinventing the wheel on a daily basis. The 5-step system gives you a steady framework you can adjust and build on. But when your customer data *does* shift, time is of the essence.

Don't just assume that everything's the way it was last year, last month, or even last week. The real power of the Undefeated Marketing System is having customer data at your fingertips. You will have such a nuanced, thorough understanding of who your customer is and what they value, you will never have the rug pulled out from under you. You'll be able to take a page out of Coca-Cola's book and adapt at a moment's notice.

FOLLOW THE FORMULA AND YOU WILL GROW

In any given political campaign, you're juggling a lot of considerations. I was hired in the 2016 election to focus only on 3 specific states—Florida, New Hampshire, and North Carolina—but I was still dealing with a lot of moving pieces. *Which voters could make the difference? What issues did they care about? Where did they spend their time? What kind of ad could cut through the marketing clutter?*

What kind of time frame were we dealing with, and what kind of budget did we have to make it work?

Add in the fact that political campaigns are fast-paced, win-or-die situations with an unavoidable "end date" and you've got a recipe for a high-intensity marketing push. Those recipes also frequently go by another name: trouble. There's a lot that can go wrong when you're dealing with that much information in such a pressure-cooker environment.

But here's the thing: all of our ads worked, either in victory or in improving Trump's outcomes, even if we didn't win every race. We had a positive return on investment in Florida and North Carolina, and in New Hampshire, we helped improve the results from previous presidential campaigns.

Why? Because we followed the 5 steps of the Undefeated Marketing System. We didn't let the pressure get to us, because we had an orderly system. That makes it a whole lot easier to keep all those balls in the air successfully.

Marketing in this day and age is complicated. That is a fact. But it doesn't have to be as mysterious as a lot of corporate marketing agencies make it. Complicated doesn't mean risky or chaotic.

Your marketing can follow a formula. It can be scientific and systematic. It can rely on messaging that's data-backed, smart, engaging, and empathetic.

If you're committed to following this formula—and if you set achievable, dynamic goals—you will easily grow your bottom line.

Once you launch your campaign, your work will always be ongoing. You're still going to run into some additional challenges, so stay on top of your customers and be ready to adapt. The next 2 chapters zoom in on 2 particular areas that will help you tap into the compound effect and send your business into the stratosphere. Chapter 7, which focuses on retargeting pools, is mostly for e-commerce and B2C businesses. (But trust me, B2B business owners can learn a lot too.)

But I want to warn you. Chapter 7 is only for the "committed" business owner that wants to do the deep, hard work to go to the next level in their business. If you're an "interested" marketer or business owner, my recommendation is to skip the next chapter. It's just not for you.

CHAPTER 7

BEYOND STEP 5: BUILD YOUR RETARGETING POOL

DEMOCRATIC CANDIDATE ANDREW GILLUM WAS LEADING Republican Ron DeSantis in the Florida governor's race by double digits only a couple of weeks before Election Day. To put it bluntly, DeSantis was looking like a serious underdog.

Here's why that was such a problem: Andrew Gillum wanted to eliminate a school scholarship program that allowed low-income parents to take their kids out of a failing public school and send them to a high-performing school of their choice. He also wanted to eliminate charter schools (schools that receive government funding but operate independently of the state public school system).

That meant that there was a threat to hundreds of thousands of poor, mostly minority kids whose parents desperately wanted them to have a better education. If Gillum won, those kids would have been pulled out of their high-performing schools and placed back in the failing schools that hadn't been teaching them properly.

To make matters worse, most of these families had *no idea* that their children's futures were on the line in this election. Why? Because Gillum hadn't put that particular education policy at the center of his campaign.

Remember when I said that politicians choose 2 or 3 issues that they care about and that align with voters' interest, and they make those the center of their campaigns? That's exactly what Gillum had done. He had talked about eliminating school choice occasionally with school unions and some supporters, but he didn't mention it often—and it certainly wasn't one of his core campaign issues. That meant that his stance on school choice was hiding under the radar.

It was entirely possible that those African American and Hispanic families with kids in the scholarship program would end up voting for Gillum—completely unaware that he was going to take away life-changing opportunities from their kids.

The Florida Education Empowerment PAC couldn't sit by and watch those parents get blindsided. So they called us in to help bring this issue to the forefront. We needed every parent to know *exactly* what they were voting for when they went into the voting booth on Election Day.

We knew we had our work cut out for us too. Gillum had a solid lead that wasn't going to be easy to overcome. But those kinds of high-octane political moments are the bread-and-butter of political marketers. So, with the looming threat of a Gillum victory, we jumped in.

In this case, Step 1 was easy. We knew exactly who our target market was. It was those parents who would be affected by the elimination of charter schools and the scholarship program. And more particularly, our voter data showed, it was the moms. They were the people who would be most fired up by this issue.

So we needed to put together a strategic plan (Step 2) that would make sure our message got in front of those moms' eyeballs. Now, stop and think about it for a second. If you're trying to reach a group of school moms, where's the best place to find them? Obviously, *the schools where their kids attend*.

We identified every charter school in the state of Florida and came up with a plan to deliver ads *only* to those geographic locations. That meant that every parent that dropped their kid off in the morning, picked their kid up in the afternoon, or came to school for a PTA meeting would see our ads.

We also made sure that we would only deliver ads to people who frequently walked into those schools. For example, we were able to exclude the FedEx drivers from the pool of voters, so they wouldn't get the ads. The only people who *would* get them were the parents, staff, and faculty, who we knew were registered voters involved in those beloved schools, day in and day out.

Next, we set out to create a brand (Step 3). We put together a video ad that spoke directly to charter school parents, calling their attention to Gillum's anti-school choice statements. Parents heard—in Gillum's own voice—that he thought their cherished schools were "less accountable" than public schools. We also called their attention to the fact that Gillum had received over $1.6 million from public school teachers' unions opposed to charter schools.

We tested the ad (Step 4) on a few schools, and we saw massive reactions. It was clear that alerting the most-concerned target voters (parents) about Gillum's stance on these issues would shift their vote.

We had a wedge issue. We had a hyper-targeted audience. And we had a message that we knew would resonate with these school-choice mom voters. In other words, we had nailed steps 1 through 4 of the Undefeated Marketing System. But Election Day was fast approaching, and we had to make sure our message reached these voters over and over. We had to drive it home and drive it hard.

So, what did we do? We launched (Step 5). And we served that ad to every single member of our 130,000-person target audience an average of *30 times.*

You heard me: 30 times.

There was no escaping our ad. There was absolutely no way that parents could ignore our message when it crossed their path multiple times a day. Whether they wanted it or not, they got our message over, and over.

Most businesses that aren't in the Fortune 200 get anxiety over spending ad dollars to serve an ad 4 or 5 times to their target customer—which is, in my opinion, barely minimal in the hyper-competitive daily frenzy of today's advertising market.

But our audience saw these political ads an average of 30 times each. You may be wondering what in the world we were thinking. Why spend money to serve the ad to the same people so many times? Isn't that overkill?

No. And here's why. Because by serving the ad that many times, we damn near guaranteed that our target voters were aware of Gillum's stance on their child's education and DeSantis's support for school choice (our brand) and remembered our ads when they walked into the voting booth.

By placing these moms into a retargeting pool once they clicked on the video to "learn more," we were able to continue to deliver ads to those parents and communicate with them over and over. Retargeting the interested parents allowed us to build a relationship with them quickly, and ultimately, it helped us win their votes.

Our campaign was the most in-depth political specific geo-targeting campaign ever. Our ad received over 3 million completed views in Florida, and it had a 25% higher completion rate than the industry average. Its click-through rate was triple the industry average. In other words, that ad got parents' attention.

The reason it was seen so many times was because we kept delivering the ad to our retargeting pool of interested parents, who needed to see it multiple times to be moved to action. And the money that we poured into getting those repeated views and clicks paid off.

Remember that double-digit lead? We did the unthinkable. We closed it in a matter of weeks. There were 8,220,561 votes cast in the gubernatorial race. DeSantis won by 32,463 votes, or 0.4 of 1% of the total vote. By the end of the election, this race that wasn't competitive at the beginning was deemed by US News and World Report to be the most competitive race in the country.

Our campaign helped turn the DeSantis boat around in the final weeks of the race. It got write-ups in newspapers and news magazines across the country, including the *Miami Herald*, the *Boston Herald*, and the *Washington Examiner*. According to the *Wall Street Journal*, "'School Choice Moms' Tipped the Governor's Florida Race." The *National Review* announced, "African-American and Latino voters whose children are enrolled in private-school-choice programs or in charter schools likely tipped the scales."

DeSantis earned the support of 18% of black female voters (our target audience for the ad campaign). That was twice as many as the Republican US senate candidate, Rick Scott (running on the same ballot), and 3 times as many as President Donald Trump earned in his first run for president. Over 100,000 black women turned out to vote for Ron DeSantis—more than 3 times his 32,463-vote margin of victory.

The unique digital strategy that we put together for the Florida Education Empowerment PAC helped make the difference in one of Florida's tightest gubernatorial races ever. It also had life-changing results for those families. Not only did these kids get to stay in their beloved schools, but DeSantis also expanded school choice programs once he was in office. Now more low-income, mostly minority kids are getting a better education in Florida.

When people denigrate my work in politics, I always remind myself of this story and this Teddy Roosevelt quote:

> It is not the critic who counts; not the man who points out how the strong man stumbles, or where the doer of deeds could have done them better. The credit belongs to the man who is actually in the arena, whose face is marred by dust and sweat and blood; who strives valiantly; who errs, who comes short again and again, because there is no effort without error and shortcoming; but who does actually strive to do the deeds; who knows great enthusiasms, the great devotions; who spends himself in a worthy cause; who at the best knows in the end the triumph of high achievement, and who at the worst, if he fails, at least fails while daring greatly, so that his place shall never be with those cold and timid souls who neither know victory nor defeat.

Are you "the man in the arena" in your own business? Do you just talk about changing things, or are you doing it? Are you a committed business owner or just an interested one?

Ultimately, we didn't just target the people we already knew would cast a vote for DeSantis. We expanded our focus to a new voter group who had a deep passion for 1 issue. We spoke directly to that passion—their kids' education—and persuaded them to vote for a candidate they wouldn't normally consider. And how did we do that? We used the 5-step Undefeated Marketing System *plus* one of the most powerful tools at marketers' disposal: the retargeting pool.

If you really want to crush your marketing, it's not enough to just reach your customers. You have to make sure you're delivering your message over and over to the interested potential new customers—and that your connection with them is growing stronger every time. (Remember, almost no one buys your product or service after seeing 1 ad.)

If you want to make sure you're getting the most out of your marketing dollars, you must use retargeting pools. They're your best tool for continuing to exponentially grow your new customers. And in this chapter, I'm going to show you exactly how they will work for your business.

WHY YOU NEED TO INVEST IN RETARGETING POOLS

Now that you've performed all 5 steps of the Undefeated Marketing System, it's time to convert the customer. But the first conversion you should be going after *isn't* always about the first sale.

Say what? Phillip, have you gone crazy?

Not at all. The first conversion you're going for isn't necessarily a sale. It's moving the customer from the point where they *recognize* your ad to *discovery* of your product or service (aka clicks). You need to convert them from a passive audience to an active customer. You must make them want to learn more about what you are offering. You must build the relationship.

The more data you have on the customer and the more creative your content, the easier it is to reach this outcome. If you can get your target to take the first step in the customer journey, you're well on your way to long-term sustained conversions.

Why?

Because in today's advertising-saturated world, you must stand out from the crowd. You need to build a real relationship with the customer, and that takes time—and trust.

Remember when we talked about how off-putting it would be to propose to someone on a first date? You have to woo them. Introduce a little charm. Get to know them. Get to understand them. After you've developed a relationship over time, *then* you can make your move.

The goal of your ads isn't to skip steps and go for a full-fledged commitment from the get-go. This is 100% a recipe for failure. The goal is to move customers into a retargeting pool so you can redeliver your message and start cultivating their connection to your brand and product or service.

Maybe you're still wondering, *What exactly* is *a retargeting pool?* It's pretty simple. Once a potential customer clicks on your ad for the first time (discovery), your marketing team must put them into a pool and continually deliver more ads to them.

Have you ever wondered why, when you look at a shirt online and don't buy it, that shirt starts following you around the internet? It starts popping up in your newsfeed and on every web page you visit. The shirt you didn't know existed until yesterday is suddenly everywhere you look. That's intentional. The apparel company has put you into their retargeting pool, in the hopes that you'll keep thinking about the brand until you cave and click "buy."

Creating retargeting pools is one of the most important marketing tools you have at your disposal. Let's say you've chugged efficiently through the 5 steps, and you have a rock-solid, innovative campaign that has tested through the roof. When you launch, it starts attracting the eyes (and clicks) you expected.

You're feeling good about the time and energy you've invested, and you're optimistic about the results. *Who needs a retargeting pool?* you think. *Why would I primarily narrow my campaign's focus to just the people who've already clicked? Isn't the goal to get more eyes on my ad, not just the same eyes? In the end, won't more eyes mean more purchases?*

Here's why that's terrible logic. Most people aren't going to see your static ad or video once, click through, and spend a ton of money. That's just not how it works in today's marketing environment.

When's the last time you saw an ad for a new company or product, clicked a link, filled your cart, and immediately checked out?

It's much more likely that you clicked through, browsed around a bit, checked out their reviews, changed your mind, and closed the tab. Or maybe you even added something to your cart, but you didn't want to pull the trigger yet until you checked with your spouse, so you closed the tab. And then you forgot about it because there are 10,000 other things going on in your life.

You're not the only shopper acting that way. In fact, according to the Baymard Institute, the average shopping cart abandonment rate is 68.81%, which accounts for $260 billion in lost orders nationwide. That's a lot of money being left on the table.

Let me ask you, do you know your cart abandonment rate? What if you could decrease your abandonment rate by 50%? How much would that be worth to you?

If you want customers to follow through and buy your product, you have to keep your brand or product at the top of their mind. It takes multiple points of contact with an ad before it sticks in a customer's brain.

The best way to make sure they'll remember you is to continually serve ads only to the people who clicked on your ad to begin with.

To advertise to get new customers is the most expensive investment you can make. Why would you focus your ad spend on running a bunch of ads and hoping that people will take notice and buy your product or service the first time they see the ad? That's the epitome of "high-hanging fruit."

You want to focus your ad spend on the easiest, lowest-hanging fruit—the people who have already clicked through on your ad and shown interest in your product or service. They're the new customers who are most likely to buy. That's why you need to put them in a retargeting pool and spend more of your marketing dollars serving ads to them.

Want me to put it more clearly? Stop setting your sights on the person who's seen your ad 8 times and still refuses to click on it. They're clearly not interested.

Know who might be? The person who clicked through to view the product on your website, added it to their cart, and then decided to not buy it. That person was curious enough to take action in the first place, so it's much easier and cheaper to capitalize on their curiosity and earn a sale.

People in your retargeting pool are the best, most convertible leads you're ever going to get in an online digital targeting environment. Without a retargeting pool, your conversion rate will be a hell of a lot lower.

We worked with an e-commerce company whose conversion rate started out really low, and they didn't utilize retargeting pools before they hired us. But over the course of several months, they managed to more than 30× their online sales. That's a *lot* in the grand scheme of revenue.

Once a potential customer clicks on your ad and enters your retargeting pool, hit them over and over and over in the span of the ad cycle. That should be enough saturation to move a potential new customer from their first click to their first purchase.

The whole point of the retargeting pool isn't to make a small profit; it's to capture new customers and build long-term relationships, which add up to a greater lifetime value for each customer.

THIS IS HOW YOU BUILD A RETARGETING POOL

A lot of people think about marketing the same way they think about fishing: they toss out a net to catch customers and haul them in for a sale. That's not *wrong*, per se, but it's not the most efficient way to build your customer base and make a profit.

If you're casting a wide net, you're going to come back empty-handed a lot of the time, or you'll come with a net filled with algae, litter, and shells. You'd be much better off using a hook with specific bait to lure a specific fish. That way, every time you get a bite, you'll know it's a fish you want to keep.

When marketing is used correctly, it helps you build an authentic, long-lasting relationship with the right customers. And why is that better than casting a wide net?

Because the best marketing creates sustainable growth without relying exclusively on your advertising budget. (You might want to highlight or write that sentence down as your North Star.)

In other words, your marketing agency should be making campaigns that are so effective that, over time, you won't even need them anymore. Your customers will become so loyal, they'll talk about you nonstop. Before you know it, you'll have hordes of excited customers that you didn't even pay ad dollars to convert knocking down your door.

To make that happen, you have to continuously build a retargeting pool for your customers. Here are the 3 steps you must follow to build a retargeting pool and start converting more customers.

1. RECOGNITION

Recognition is simple. It's when your potential customer or client recognizes your ad for the first time. That's it. They haven't clicked on it. They haven't bought anything. They've just seen your ad, and they know your brand, product, or service exists.

Think of recognition as the top part of your sales funnel. Thanks to the Undefeated Marketing System, you've identified what motivates your customers or clients to action (Step 1), come up with a strategic marketing plan (Step 2) to effectively get your brand (Step 3) in front of their eyes, and you've tested (Step 4) to make sure you've mitigated as much risk as possible. Then, you launch (Step 5), and you deliver your data-backed ads to everybody in your target market.

When you deliver those ads, what you're looking for initially is recognition.

Customers will scroll online and see your ad. Then, maybe they'll keep scrolling. The next day, they will see your ad again. It will seem vaguely familiar, but maybe they'll keep scrolling.

A potential customer or client will have to see your ad multiple times before they recognize your brand. That's why it's so important to keep delivering your ads to that target audience. (It's also one reason it's more expensive to convert new customers than to focus on the ones you already have. You might have to deliver an ad to the same customer many times before they click.)

The recognition step is all about breaking through the clutter. That's why you need emotional, attention-grabbing, data-backed creative content and videos. You're trying to hook your potential customers and clients so they want to know more.

The faster you can get them to take notice of your brand, product, or service, the faster you can move them along their customer journey and get them into your retargeting pool.

Here's a good example. Remember the organic dental, skincare, and makeup client I talked about in Chapter 2—the ones who were able to pivot so well during the coronavirus pandemic? Well, recently, we worked with them to build a holiday campaign that successfully utilized retargeting pools to help them stand out from all the other holiday marketing competition.

We looked at their customer data (Step 1), which told us that the target market was looking for solutions to their problems that helped them incorporate more organic products into their everyday lives. So we built a strategic plan designed to drive new traffic to their sales funnel (Step 2), and created compelling ads for their top-performing social media platforms (Step 3) that positioned our client's products as the ideal solutions to their problems. Then we tested a bunch of those ads (Step 4). The one that broke through all the clutter was an ad featuring a charcoal-based toothpowder called Dirty Mouth.

The ad was a 6-second digital video ad showcasing the product's label, the charcoal powder, and a very distinctive message: "Dirty Mouth is the new clean mouth."

That slogan immediately piqued customers' interest because it was so perplexing, and it immediately highlighted one of the product's unique features. If you brush with charcoal, your mouth will turn black—but afterward, your teeth will be sparkling clean. The unusual language of the ad—Dirty Mouth is the new clean mouth—was super-recognizable and made the product stand out.

When we launched the ad campaign (Step 5), we knew beyond a shadow of a doubt that "Dirty Mouth is the new clean mouth" was catchy enough to bring our client's target customers from recognition (seeing the ad and knowing the brand exists) to discovery (being curious enough to click on the ad).

2. DISCOVERY

The second step—discovery—happens when you've successfully created enough curiosity for this potential customer. It's when they say, "I want to discover what this product is," and click your link to find out more.

That "discovery" click is the first conversion every business owner should be looking for.

Why?

Because now you can put them in the retargeting pool. Something in the ad piqued their interest, so you know they are more likely to become your customer.

You can move them out of the large ocean of your recognition-phase target audience. Now they can go into a much smaller pond of interested potential customers, and you can deliver your ads to them over and over. Why? Because people have a million things going on in their lives, and buying your product or service might not be at the top of their list. But the more you can bring it to the top of their mind, the more likely they are to remember it and act on it.

If they don't bite after a couple of weeks, then you can drop them from your retargeting pool. Their interest was probably fleeting. But many will click again, and your next goal is to move them to *engagement* (a purchase).

In the case of the "Dirty Mouth is the new clean mouth" campaign, we saw that the ad got an above-average click-through rate, so we knew it was creating enough curiosity to drive customers to the discovery stage.

But once your customers or clients have clicked through, what can you do in the discovery phase to move them to engagement? For this particular client, we used our Step 1 customer data to brand their website in a way that spoke directly to their target customers' needs.

Once potential customers clicked through to the website, they learned about the benefits of using organic charcoal toothpaste through a blog post called "3 Ways to Better Your Dental and Overall Health," which helped convince them that this was a good solution for their everyday concerns. We also emphasized 5-star reviews of the toothpowder, which gave potential customers social proof of the product's effectiveness.

Because the 5-step Undefeated Marketing System had given us a firm, data-backed understanding of the target customers, we knew what kinds of information would encourage them to make a purchase.

Let me give you another example of how retargeting pools can help move people from discovery to conversion. This one comes from the political marketing world. We saw the power of the retargeting pool in action when we were working with a Fortune 200 healthcare company that needed help getting the attention of Congress.

People care about healthcare, but most of the time, it doesn't exactly make for riveting news. Who wants to hear about insurance premiums when they could be reading about the latest political scandal or celebrity cancel-culture gaffe? So, understandably, complex healthcare legislation has a hard time competing for attention in a sea of cable news and front-page favorites.

Our job was to find a way to break through and get the issue in front of legislators' eyes. And not only that, but to make the issue stick with them.

As you can probably guess by now, we followed the 5 steps to the letter. By the time we launched (Step 5), we had a well-tested (Step 4) batch of emotional content (Step 3) that we could strategically deliver to legislators (Step 2) in order to tug at their heartstrings in all the right ways (Step 1). In other words, we had a winning recipe for the high-value, high-frequency campaign we needed.

But this chapter isn't just about the recipe. It's about the secret sauce—the retargeting pool. And that secret sauce was critical to our strategy with this client. To make sure we got the attention of our audience—the members of Congress who could make or break this legislation—we retargeted the hell out of anyone who was willing to click our ads (discovery). Once they were in the retargeting pool, we pushed more content their way and deepened their understanding of the issue.

By the end of the campaign, we had over 8.5 million video views, over 90,000 clicks to site (discovery!), and 2.6 million social media engagements. As a result, our client saw a 33% increase in interaction with their brand, and people who came into contact with our ad were 4 times more likely to recall it.

The impact was so large that any time our client walked into a US senator's office, that senator and their staff said, "Oh, yeah! I've seen your ad." They immediately knew who our client was, what the issue was, and what was at stake, right off the bat. In fact, several senators and congressmen and congresswomen told our clients just how big an impact the campaign had in their districts.

Obviously, in this example, there's no literal sale at stake. But retargeting works the exact same way in corporate marketing as it does in political marketing. Once people have discovered your brand and entered the retargeting pool, a constant delivery of ads helps your brand stay at the forefront of their brain.

The first time they visit your site, they may not click "buy." But once they've researched your product, thought about it for a few days, and have seen 5 or 6 ads reminding them of how much they liked your products, they're much more likely to come back and make that first purchase.

3. ENGAGEMENT

Let's say your customer has clicked on your ad (discovery) and entered the retargeting pool. You've delivered ads to them for a week, and now they've clicked again. They're back on your site, and they're much more familiar with your brand, products, or services.

This is the moment when they start engaging with your brand. They might look through your website and get to know more about your product range. They might watch your videos or read some of your testimonials.

That full package of data-backed branding that you created as part of Step 3? Here's where it really comes into play. Your data-backed ads intrigued your potential customers enough to get them to your website or e-commerce store, but now the rest of the brand has to *engage* them.

Think back to that national pest control client I mentioned in Chapter 1 who used the Undefeated Marketing System to achieve the highest monthly sales record in their 35-year history. We ran ads and used a retargeting pool to keep delivering ads to potential customers who entered the discovery phase. But we knew that we had to engage those potential customers if we wanted to move them to conversion.

How did we do that? When they visited our client's website, they saw a video on the landing page, talking about the family-owned business and their charity work. They saw technicians in clean uniforms. They saw that they could bundle their services (which, if you recall, made these particular clients feel smart). And they saw that the company used green products. Basically, they saw that everything about that pest control company's brand matched their needs and values.

We didn't just throw a bunch of videos up on the site and call it day. During Step 3 of our 5-step system, we created the brand in a very strategic way. Why? Because once you get people in the engagement phase of the retargeting pool, you want them to look at your brand and say, "Wow. This company is different."

When your customers are engaged, they're more likely to add items to their cart (or reach out for more information about your services).

Now let's say your potential customers abandon the cart. For business owners without a retargeting pool, that would be the kiss of death. The fish would have slipped off the hook and wriggled back into the "target audience" ocean.

But if you have a retargeting pool, cart abandonment is a much smaller problem. You can keep delivering that potential customer or client ads to entice them to come back and engage with your brand some more. You'd be surprised at how effective that constant delivery of ads can be.

For example, we noticed that our organic products client had a relatively high cart abandonment rate with their holiday campaign. So, what did we do to make sure those customers came back, engaged, and made their purchase? We retargeted them with different ads. This time, we delivered them real customer testimonials, offered a 5% discount, and provided a free-shipping code. In other words, we incentivized the cart abandoners during the engagement phase to get them back on board.

And what were the results of this particular campaign? Our clients saw a 31% increase in year-over-year revenue and a website conversion rate almost 3 times the industry average. They also saw a huge return on their ad spend (between 3× and 5.3×, depending on the platform). Now, just think about that. If you could spend $100,000 on an ad campaign and get between $300,000 and $530,000 in return, that's a huge number. Retargeting pools work.

When you've successfully engaged your customers, you can finally move them to conversion. They're finally willing to buy everything they've added to the cart. That's great—you've got a new customer. But this is the moment when a lot of business owners get complacent. They think they've achieved their goal by getting a conversion.

Let me tell you, now is your chance to turn that first purchase into a lifetime of purchases by building a relationship with that customer.

HOW YOU CAN BUILD A LIFETIME RELATIONSHIP WITH YOUR CUSTOMERS

Once you've got 1 sale under your belt, your next goal is to build a relationship with and retain that customer. Customer repurchase is the second-highest ROI in the game (surpassed only by the next step in a customer's journey: raving fandom).

To quote my friend and marketing genius Jay Abraham, building a customer relationship is "guaranteed to bring you bigger buys, better buys, more profitable buys, no-cost buys, more consistent buys, more loyal buyers, more referring buyers, each and every month—from NOW on."

If you're starting over and trying to convert new customers with every sale you make, you're doing it wrong, and you will eventually go broke. Your goal should be motivating repeat customers who've connected with your brand, enjoyed their purchases, and want to come back for more. You want to increase your existing customers' lifetime value by building a sustainable relationship with them.

Here's an example of a company that's great at building relationships with their customers (and improving their lifetime value). When I was starting my career in the 1990s, I had multiple people tell me, "You need to buy all your work clothes at Nordstrom." I asked why, and they said, "Because you can wear those clothes for 2 years, and if anything happens to them, you can take it back, and they'll give you a full refund, no matter what. No questions asked." At the time, I didn't have a lot of money, and that policy made me feel like I had a risk-free buy. So I ended up buying all my clothes from Nordstrom for years.

One day, I decided I wanted to test their policy out. I had a button-down shirt that I had been wearing for a few years, and I went to the store to return it. Not to get too graphic, but it had some dirt stains around the neck from when I was wearing a tie, and—well, let's just say that you could tell that this shirt had been used.

I walked up to the cashier and said, "This shirt doesn't fit." The guy looked at me and said, "When'd you buy it?" And I said, "I can't remember."

Then he looked at it—straight at the neck stain. And then he looked at me. And then looked back at the neck stain. And then looked at me. And then he said, "All right. I'll get you a refund."

It was a little devious for me to take an old shirt back, but the cashier's response was the best possible way to get me back in that store. The fact is, I probably spent over $10,000 with Nordstrom in the '90s—because they did everything they could to show me that they cared about building a relationship with me. I didn't feel too bad about returning that $80 2-year-old shirt. In the end, they created a raving fan in me and they got all my money.

When you're a company with a repeat customer who's sold on your products or services, that's a golden opportunity. Don't limit your possibilities by focusing too closely on individual sales. Focus on building a relationship with that customer, and I promise you, you'll see a higher lifetime value.

Make your repeat customers an asset for your brand and turn them into full-fledged brand advocates. Turn those customers into raving fans and let them become your marketers.

I practice what I preach. The whole reason we use the Undefeated Marketing System at Win BIG Media is so we can eliminate the risk of the business owner every step of the way and put their needs first. Every contract people sign with us is month-to-month, and when clients work with us on their strategic plan, there's a money-back guarantee in case they're not happy with the plan. We do all these things to make sure that we build trust and a stronger relationship with our client from the get-go.

When you're trying to determine what will create raving fans, ask yourself: What does your company already do that might make a difference to your customers? How are you already giving back to the community? What are the core values of your organization, and how might those resonate with your customers and clients?

Here's a great example from one of our apparel clients. Their brand was centered around comfort, and they came to us to create a campaign around providing comfort to their local homeless population. That was a cause near and dear to their hearts, and it was also one that they knew would resonate with their customers. So we pushed out a video that focused on employees preparing boxes of free clothing and delivering them to local shelters.

Here's the thing. That video wasn't intended to draw in new customers. It was intended to deepen this company's relationship with its existing customers. By highlighting the brand's values in an authentic way that was also meaningful to customers, they were able to connect with their customers and move one step closer to creating raving fans.

HOW POST-PURCHASE RAVING FANS CAN SEND YOUR SALES THROUGH THE ROOF

What do the most successful companies in America have in common?

They all have brands that inspire intense loyalty.

Look at Apple, Amazon, and Starbucks. They barely have to market themselves because their customers will do it for them.

Don't get me wrong. Of course those companies have huge ad budgets. But their marketing isn't focused solely on paid media. If you want to become a mainstay for your customers, you need to place just as much emphasis on customer experience (and, if you have the money, public relations) as you do on your ad spend.

Loyal raving fans are your free marketing machine. Don't believe me? Then maybe you'll believe Arthur Blank.

10 to 15 years ago, when you attended a concert or sporting event, 2 things happened every time you walked up to the concession stand: bad food and high prices.

But then, innovation and disruption started to enter into the marketplace. A few years ago, stadiums started to address the "bad arena food" situation by letting upscale restaurants and high-profile chefs bring their culinary expertise to big-time concerts and sporting events.

That was great. But guess what didn't change? Prices! In fact, prices didn't just remain expensive, they became astronomical. Ever bought an $18 beer at a game? WTF?

One sports owner decided to put the power back in the consumer's hands and disrupt a market prime for innovation. That man was Atlanta Falcons owner Arthur Blank, who likes to be called "Uncle Arthur."

When Blank opened the new Mercedes-Benz Stadium a few years ago, he was adamant that "fans come first." He applied that mantra to everything from inexpensive seats to affordable food. This guy believes that a family of 4 shouldn't go bankrupt by attending a single football game. Blank is my hero.

So, how low-cost is the food at the Mercedes-Benz Stadium? The hot dogs cost $1.50, the big ATL burgers are $7.50, and the large waffle ice cream cones cost $4.50.

Even though the money-obsessed, needle-nosed nerds in the accounting office recommended Blank slightly raise food prices 2 years later, he said no. Instead, he did something even crazier. Instead of raising prices or keeping them flat, Blank cut them again!

"Uncle Arthur" branded his legacy by putting fans first in a way that built a deep and loyal connection. And do you know what this outlier strategy got him? Concession sales at Mercedes-Benz Stadium grew by 50%, and 10% more fans entered the stadium an hour before kickoff (which also increased food and beverage sales).

Blank identified his biggest customer frustration and capitalized on it to build a deeper connection and convert more sales. He didn't have to spend a gazillion dollars marketing that disruptive innovation. The media and fans did it for him, for free!

As the legendary marketer and author of *Fanocracy*, David Meerman Scott, says, "The most powerful marketing force in the world isn't social media, email blasts, search ads, or even those 15-second commercials before a YouTube video. It's fandom."

Remember in the last section when I talked about the lifetime value of customers? That's what fandom is all about. If your typical customer spends $55, and a repeat customer spends $110, just think about how much a raving fan might spend over the course of their lifetime. You could double, triple, or even 10× that number over the span of years. And it's 1,000 times easier to get a sale from a loyal customer or client than to prospect for a new one.

If you can take the lifetime value of your customer from $55 to $1,000, you're going to make more money than you've ever made before. You're also going to continue giving back to that customer at a level you've never done before. Good karma equals a successful life.

Raving fans will be so over the moon with your brand, that they'll become your biggest advocates. They'll tell all their friends and family (word of mouth). They'll wear your merchandise proudly (free brand campaign). They'll post about you on social media (free advertising).

Know what that means?

You'll be able to bring even more new customers into the fold without spending a dollar because they'll want the great products and services their friends and family brag about all the time. Raving fans' loyalty is the best way to get other people into your sales funnel and add even more lifetime value—and it doesn't cost you a dime.

Remember when I told you that you should model big companies because they're ahead of the curve when it comes to investing in and following customer data? It's also a good rule of thumb to pay attention to how these companies create raving fans. Here are 2 exceptional examples to consider.

During the coronavirus, the marketing team for Popeyes really stepped up to the plate. Almost immediately, they ran a "Fried Chicken and Chill" campaign, as a riff on the "Netflix and Chill" trend. They gave away a month of free Netflix to the first 3 million customers. That didn't make Popeyes any extra money right off the bat. But here's what it did do: it provided value to their loyal customers, strengthened their loyalty, and let the company gather more data about their customers' preferences. In the long run (See the theme here? There's no get-rich-quick pill.), they made upwards of 8 figures in profit just by giving first.

The athletic apparel company Lululemon is the second "lesson-worthy" example. They frequently go into the communities that their stores are in and give products away to local yoga instructors. They take pictures of the instructors wearing the gear, and they put posters all over the store of these "local influencers."

The local yoga instructor gets excited by the thought that she's on the store's wall of fame, and she's proud of her connection to the brand. She starts buying all her clothes there. Then, in class, dozens of people see the instructor wearing Lululemon gear and hear her gushing about the brand. Word spreads, then the company starts selling even more yoga apparel to people who don't even practice yoga.

That's how you build a $46 billion brand. That's the power of raving fan marketing.

No matter what disruption is happening in the world, no matter what's going on or what the economy's like, if your customers see you as giving, trusting, and authentic, they're going to stay with you forever.

YOUR MARKETING TEAM SHOULD WORK THEMSELVES OUT OF A JOB

The mission of your marketing agency shouldn't only be to spend your money building a new customer base forever. It should also be to build loyalty. In fact, it should be every marketer's goal to work themselves out of a job. They should want your company to have such a loyal demand and such crazy, raving fans that you don't even need your marketing firm anymore. In an ideal world, your raving fans *are* your marketers. Ultimately, that's what I'm trying to achieve with all my clients.

Here's the bottom line: you need a retargeting pool if you want to reduce risk with your marketing, spend less money, build trust, increase lifetime value, and create raving fans. And you need raving fans if you want to stop wasting marketing dollars and tap into compound growth.

The retargeting pool was a key part of our win against Andrew Gillum in the Florida governor's race. In an election that saw over 8 million votes cast, our unique marketing strategy made the difference. We found new, persuadable voters who wouldn't typically support a Republican candidate and delivered highly emotional messages to them *over and over*.

The continual delivery of ads helped us build a relationship with key voters. And, in the end, we helped secure a long-shot victory for Ron DeSantis, and we ultimately kept low-income Florida kids in their safe, high-quality schools. Without retargeting pools, none of that would have been possible.

It also wouldn't have been possible without 1 other tactic: going negative.

CHAPTER 8

COMPARATISING...AKA "GOING NEGATIVE" (AGAIN)

IF YOU'VE READ MY FIRST BOOK, *FIRE THEM NOW*, YOU know that I wrote an entire chapter about how effective negative ads are at influencing voter and consumer behavior. You may even remember the story I told about how every election, you hear candidates say, "I'm not going to run any negative ads. This is going to be a clean campaign." Then cut to 2 months later, and all you see are ads telling you why their opponent isn't fit to clean a pig's trough.

Politicians don't decide to run negative ads because they're vicious, bloodthirsty people. They don't relish slinging mud or stirring up their opponent's anger (or at least most of them don't). There is only one reason politicians decide to run negative ads: they work.

In *Fire Them Now*, I made the case that all business owners need to "go negative" in their advertising. But I quickly learned that a lot of business owners aren't comfortable with the idea of "going negative" in corporate advertising. Most of them are worried that they're going to offend their customers and drive away business. I get it. I face this kind of resistance from business owners all the time. But in my opinion, they're making a huge mistake.

"Going negative" doesn't mean you have to go in for the kill. It just requires you to *focus on drawing comparisons with your competition so that customers see you as the better choice.* That's why I've reframed the concept and coined a new word: *comparatising* (short for "comparative advertising").

I've been a part of comparison ads in politics for over 24 years, and I can tell you from firsthand experience, when it comes to marketing, comparatising can be a slam-dunk, especially if you're trying to disrupt your competition. Here's a great example that shows comparatising in action.

Recently, we were advising on a governor's race in the Midwest. Right before a statewide televised debate, a scandal broke about our candidate's opponent. It had just hit the headlines that he had plagiarized several of his education plans.

This was a huge opportunity. In politics, any time you get the chance to steer the narrative, you take it. We knew that this scandal had the power to push our candidate to victory. We just had to get the message out to voters at lightning speed.

We used the data and research we had already gathered about our target voters (Step 1) and determined how this information could fit within our strategic plan (Step 2). We needed to make sure that this scandal hit so hard that the debate moderators couldn't ignore it. We wanted our opponent on the ropes, struggling to defend himself. We wanted to push this information into prime time. Why? So every target voter would go to the polls knowing just how badly our opponent had behaved.

To make that happen, we had to get creative with the targeting and timing of the campaign. We targeted the 10 largest local TV newsrooms in the state and a 3-mile radius around the physical location where the upcoming debate would take place.

Next, we had to create the brand message and the creative (Step 3) that would draw attention to the scandal. How did we do that? We created a website around the brand, which gave interested voters all the facts about the scandal. Our ads poked fun at the opponent, gave him a catchy nickname, and encouraged voters to visit the site to learn more.

Then we speed-tested our ads (Step 4), linked them to the website, and realized they were spot-on effective in rousing voters' curiosity. That meant the campaign was ready to launch by the morning of the debate (Step 5). We delivered digital ads in our concentrated areas before, during, and after the debate, and we dominated our opponent's name on all search platforms.

In less than 12 hours, our ads had made more than 750,000 impressions, and more than 30 news outlets had reported on the scandal. Our efforts were so effective, the very first question in the statewide televised debate was about our opponent's plagiarism misstep.

This was a huge victory because it allowed our candidate to take control of the debate. And do you want to know the best part? We saw those massive results after only spending $5,000.

Here's why comparatising ads are so powerful: they grab people's attention and allow you to take charge in an uber-competitive marketplace.

Why? Because, love 'em or hate 'em, comparatising ads make people *feel* something. Media feeds on drama, and the more drama you can dredge up, the more likely it is that your message will spread.

Comparatising ads are a hugely powerful advertising tactic, and businesses routinely underestimate their effectiveness. When you do comparatising right, nothing will help you see faster returns.

I'm not the original person to bring this concept to corporate America, but I might be its biggest advocate. Just look at the name of my first book. My friend James Altucher, who knows business like the back of his hand, even sat me down one day and said, "Phillip, *Fire Them Now* is just too negative for a book title. You've got to be more uplifting for your next one."

"That's why I chose *The Undefeated Marketing System*," I replied matter-of-factly.

"But hold on," James said. "Undefeated is a double negative."

He had a point, but I didn't care. I stuck with it because comparatising is in my blood. I know it's not for everyone, but I also know that it works.

Here's the thing. Negative political ads are so brutal because they have to be. Voters have to make an either-or choice, so political marketers are fighting tooth and nail to make sure their candidate comes out on top. It's nasty, and we like it.

But corporate advertising isn't an either-or situation. Consumers make lots of different buying decisions, for different reasons, at different times. You can create strong comparisons without offending or losing any customers.

Comparatising ads in corporate advertising don't have to go for the jugular the way political ads do. Instead, if you want to execute successful comparatising, here's what you have to do: draw a deep distinction between your brand and the competition without offending your customer base. And I'm going to show you how.

Trust me, *people respond very strongly when they see your product or service as more effective, valuable, or useful than the competition.*

Think about it. When you're standing in the grocery store aisle, comparing 2 different kinds of soap, what influences your decision? One soap might smell better than the other. You might think one cleans better than the other. One might have healthier ingredients than the other. Whatever your deciding factor is, at its core, your choice is about one thing: *which one is better?*

Comparatising in a strategic and targeted manner can be huge for businesses looking for an outlier strategy to increase their market share and consumer base. Let me explain why.

HERE IS HOW TO OVERCOME YOUR MARKETING FEARS

About a month after *Fire Them Now* came out, I did an interview for *Inc.* about the power of negative advertising. I explained exactly why it works so well, and I even made the caveat that I've just given you: your goal in corporate marketing is comparison, not annihilation.

They posted the article, but a few days later, they took it down. Why? Because they were scared shitless to do anything that offended anyone. Just *talking* about negative advertising made *Inc.* turn their tail and run the other way.

Don't think I'm picking on *Inc.* They're far from alone in this. In fact, they were probably just reflecting the fears of their readers' clickbait habit. I see it all the time. Business owners are so scared to take chances with their marketing that they avoid anything remotely innovative at all costs.

In today's "don't rock the boat" business culture, CEOs are so afraid to run comparatising ads on their competitors that they won't even consider it. Instead, they put up generic crap in their marketing that doesn't offend anyone and doesn't convert customers at a high level either.

But guess what? That generic crap also doesn't excite your customers. And if your marketing doesn't make your customer excited, you will lose money and then blame someone for a bad marketing campaign.

I get it too. You've spent so much time and effort building your business, you don't want to do anything that might jeopardize what you've built. You're petrified that comparatising ads might reflect poorly back on you, and no one wants to come across as a bully. But if there is 1 thing I want you to take away from the chapter, it's this:

There is very little risk when running comparatising marketing campaigns.

The common misconception that leads CEOs and business owners away from comparison advertising is the idea that you have to go full boar, abandon all taste, and totally disparage your competition. That's a low-IQ game.

No one is telling you to run an ad where you say, "My competitor makes worthless products, offers appalling customer service, and has a CEO that does morally questionable things after-hours." That's a recipe for disaster. And probably some lawsuits.

Remember, the stakes of political campaigns are different. In politics, we're prepared to beat people over the head with base-ball bats (and to be beaten). Corporate comparatising is all about nuance. You have to be smart about it. You have to draw distinctions that resonate with customers but don't offend.

For example, Wendy's has mastered the art of comparatising on social media. Their Twitter account has spawned a hugely loyal fan base just by embracing the power of comparatising. When the International House of Pancakes (IHOP) joked that they were going to change their name to International House of Burgers, someone tweeted, "So @Wendys, u gonna let @IHOb sell burgers on your block? Thought you were the OG?"

Wendy's replied, "Not really afraid of the burgers from a place that decided pancakes were too hard."

It's funny, brutal, and brilliant. Let me ask you something. Are you offended by that? Do you plan to boycott Wendy's?

There are so many proven cases of corporate America comparatising in a strategic, smart way that makes their customers even more loyal. It has absolutely no downside. And yet 99.9% of business owners are too scared to try it.

But just think, if comparatising were really that risky, why would so many major companies, like Wendy's (and the others you'll see in this chapter) do it? They wouldn't. They're spending millions of dollars on their marketing, and they wouldn't do anything that would jeopardize their brand or their business.

Want to know a secret I've learned over the years? Modeling successful ideas is the smartest way to do anything in this world. For example, I've modeled my entire investment strategy on the strategies of really smart people. I figure out where they're investing their money and go invest in the same thing. And it's worked for 25-plus years.

Why do anything different when it comes to marketing? Look at what all the big companies are doing with their marketing. They're using customer data to put out cutting-edge creative marketing, and they're not guessing. They're doing what they're doing because they've put millions of dollars into research. They know, beyond a shadow of a doubt, what will motivate their customer base.

Even if you don't have a $390 million advertising budget like Wendy's, you *do* have the power to observe, take notes, and model your own marketing on big companies' expertise. When you pay attention, you'll see that comparatising is one of the best ways to stand out in a very crowded field.

As a business owner or marketer reading this book, you do not have to spend millions of dollars to figure this out. Be smart. Find out what your customer cares about. Use that information to find the differences between yourself and your competitors. By using this 5-step marketing system, you can then crush your competition.

Remember, you're not just making some random, wild comparison and hoping it works. If you've followed the 5-step formula, you *know* what's going to resonate with your customers and clients. You'll know what distinctions matter to them and what will motivate them. To return to our earlier example, if you're selling soap, you'll know whether your target customers care more about the smell, cleaning power, or ingredients.

And thanks to the Undefeated Marketing System, you'll be able to minimize your risk at every step of the way. By the time you're ready to launch your marketing campaign, you can be certain the comparatising will hit its target.

TO WIN THE MARKETING BATTLE, YOU MUST FIND THE RIGHT "RIVAL"

The first step of comparatising is to find your "rival." Who are you going to draw your comparison with?

The most successful target isn't necessarily your most obvious competitor. For example, we work with a nutritional supplement company that makes protein powders, bars, and shakes. If we only thought of comparatising as a direct attack on the competition, we would have looked at who had the biggest slice of their market share and started aiming for that particular company (probably GNC). But when we looked at our target consumer data, we knew that approach wouldn't bring our client the best ROI.

So we dug into the research (Step 1), and as you might expect from a nutritional supplement company, their customer base was health-conscious. They were also 4 times more likely to be vegetarian or vegan than the average American. These particular customers also based their purchasing decisions more on quality than price.

But here's where it got interesting. We found that 77% of their customers avoided drinking soda. That's nearly 2 times more than the average American.

Bingo. That information offered us a clear "enemy" for us to build our comparatising campaign around: soda. And here's the kicker. We would not be offending any customer or name-dropping any other brands.

We built our strategic marketing plan (Step 2) and content (Step 3) around all the customer insights we gained during Step 1. Then, during our testing phase (Step 4), we developed a mix of 10 different ads with messaging we knew would resonate with our health-conscious target customers. 9 of those ads were positive, and 1 was a comparatising ad.

After weeks of testing, the results were staggering. *The comparatising ad outperformed the positive ads by a huge margin.* Compared to the highest-ranking positive ad (the number 2 ad overall), the comparatising ad got nearly 2 times as many clicks and had a 20% higher conversion rate. Basically, comparatising blew positive advertising out of the water. The comparatising ad generated far more action and conversions.

Now let's talk more about the copy on that comparatising ad because I think you'll be surprised at just how benign a "negative" ad can seem. The ad read, "Drinks That Fuel Your Body—Unlike Those Other Guys." At the top, next to the "fuel" line, we showed a picture of our client's product in a high-quality, reusable cup. At the bottom, next to the "other guys" reference, we included a picture of a crushed aluminum soda can. In an instant, people looking at the ad could see the comparison: a healthy, quality "fueling" drink versus a crumpled, cheap, unhealthy soda.

Come on. Even the most easily offended person in the world wouldn't be offended by that ad.

The negativity was subtle, but it was powerful. It showed the target customers all the ways our client's brand stood out from their competitors. And surprise, surprise—all those strong suits just "happened" to align with our target customers' core values.

When you're comparatising, you're not screaming until you're blue in the face about how terrible your competitors are. You're letting your audience come to their own conclusions. That way, they feel more ownership over their choices.

Think about it this way. Every business transaction is a negotiation, and in a negotiation, both parties like to feel ownership. No one likes to be railroaded. So let your customer come to the table and choose you.

According to Chris Voss, former FBI negotiator and bestselling author of *Never Split the Difference*, there are 2 words that immediately transform any negotiation: "That's right."

When people have epiphanies ("That's right!"), they feel like they've listened to your claims, evaluated them, and made their own decision. That's way more powerful than just telling your customer, "Listen to me. I'm better than the other guy." Comparatising is all about getting people to say, "That's right," when they see your ad.

Here's something a lot of business owners and marketers don't realize. *There's a huge difference between "that's right" and "you're right."*

Imagine that a customer's just watched your comparison ad. They nod and say, "Yes, you're right. I should stop eating so much junk food."

A lot of business owners would think that's a major success. After all, didn't the customer come around and see things your way?

Not at all.

Chances are, your customers already know that they shouldn't eat so much junk food. You being right isn't going to make them take action.

Voss explains it this way. When you tell someone "you're right," they get a happy smile and leave you alone. "You're right" is a great way to get people to stop bothering you. *But it doesn't mean someone has agreed to your position.*

Just think about it. How many times have you had an argument with your spouse where you say, "Okay, you're right, *but...*"

"You're right" is a way to keep the conversation going or to push it aside for a while. It's not a resolution.

So, when a customer sees your comparison ads, you're not trying to drag them to the conclusion that you're right. You're trying to get them to draw the conclusion for themselves. You want them to say, "That's right. Those other drinks *are* terrible quality."

A "that's right" epiphany is going to make them much more likely to buy.

It may sound like a subtle distinction, but trust me, the results between those 2 statements couldn't be more different. "You're right" versus "that's right" is the difference between telling a customer what to do versus truly connecting with them on their terms.

Remember, your goal is to build an emotional connection in a largely unemotional consumer world. A successful comparatising ad brings the customer curiosity. It makes them want to discover your brand. Comparatising is 1 of the best ways to grab someone's attention, as long as you're helping them come to a realization about your "enemy."

In a nutshell, comparatising is about carefully using the power of comparison to create underdog status with consumers, engage with your audience, build your following, and craft an environment where a customer draws their own negative conclusions about your competitor. That way, the customer chooses you, all by themselves.

WHY YOU SHOULD ALWAYS PUNCH UP AND NEVER PUNCH DOWN

When you're the underdog in the marketplace, comparatising is one of your greatest tools. If you can gain ground by showing yourself in a better light than your competitors, you should do it. Not only does it put you in the same league as industry leaders, but it also shows that you have the potential to rise above those leaders. In *Fire Them Now*, I described this as "David taking on Goliath."

We had a David and Goliath situation with one of our clients, a sports apparel company, and we knew that comparatising would be the perfect solution. After running a Customer Insights Report for them (Step 1), we realized that their biggest issue wasn't that they didn't know their customer. It was that their customers didn't know them.

We desperately needed to increase their brand awareness and retargeting pool, so we asked ourselves, "What's the fastest way to increase recognition amongst a competitive target audience?" Comparatising.

We made this the centerpiece of our strategic marketing plan

(Step 2) and created a comparatising campaign (Step 3) that showed our target customer how superior the quality and look of our client's apparel was.

Because we were looking to make a splash, we didn't just punch up, we punched *way* up. We decided to take aim at some of the biggest apparel companies on the market—but in a way that didn't mention their name and wouldn't offend customers. Our 3 test ads (Step 4) riffed on the taglines of popular companies like Nike and Forever 21.

All of the ads performed well, but one shot ahead of the rest. It had *7 times* as many engagements than the second-highest-performing ad:

Still buying your clothes from a shoe company?

Just don't do it.

Not bad, huh? If you smiled reading that shot at Nike, you get my ultimate point about comparatising.

The ad was short and to the point. But in just a few words, it spoke to our target customers' core desires for comfort, independence, recognition, and being a trendsetter (all drawn from Step 1). More importantly, the ad let customers have an epiphany: *Why am I buying clothes from a shoe company that makes cheap crap?*

Even in the testing phase, that ad got our client conversions. It had an ROI 3 times better than the client's typical ads. So, by the time we launched (Step 5), we knew that punching up was going to pay off.

Nike is such a behemoth, I'm not sure they noticed. But for our fledgling David of a client, it paid big bucks to challenge the industry giant. And we did it in a smart, nuanced way. There was no name-calling. No mudslinging. No blood on the ground. But everyone who saw that ad (the target customer who valued high-quality apparel) knew who we were gunning for. The comparison we made was crystal clear.

Okay, Phillip, you may be saying. *But what if I'm not the underdog? What if I'm the top dog in my field? Can I still use comparatising to my advantage?*

The answer is still yes, but it's trickier. My mantra is "Always punch up, never punch down." If you're #1, you can still use it, but you have to proceed with caution. Imagine how consumers would feel if McDonald's suddenly ran an ad against Mom and Pop's Burger Emporium? It would probably have the opposite effect and inspire people to flock to Mom and Pop's.

Companies like Bud Light and Miller Lite, who are at the top of their market, still think it's worth it to run negative ads against each other. Like I said earlier, if you're going to go negative, you have to be smart about it, and that's even truer if you're already on top.

WHEN YOU'RE EXPLAINING, YOU'RE LOSING

There's an old axiom in politics: "When you're explaining, you're losing."

We can probably all think of a time when we've heard a politician try to defend themselves against an outrageous attack, but instead, they just dig the hole deeper. While trying to explain, they repeat the attack, which only sears the accusation deeper into voters' brains.

Successful comparatising puts you in charge of the narrative and puts your competitor on the defensive.

Does it always work? No. But it works enough to do it. That's why Bud Light's marketing team came up with a comparatising campaign on Coors Light and Miller Lite that will go down as legendary.

Bud Light made a major advertising coup by targeting Coors Light and Miller Lite for using corn syrup in their brewing process. (Bud Light uses rice instead of corn syrup.)

Why? The corn industry is under a major threat and has received a ton of bad press from health advocates and the anti-sugar lobby. Bud Light went all-in and spent an estimated $50 million on a comparatising campaign, including $13 million to run an ad during the Super Bowl. It was a strong play.

True story: when my wife saw the Bud Light Super Bowl "corn syrup" ad, she looked at me and said, "I'm done drinking Miller Lite." Bud Light clearly knew what the data said about how to reach their customers.

MillerCoors, the parent company to Coors Light and Miller Lite, knew they couldn't take the attack lying down, so they immediately filed a lawsuit against Anheuser-Busch, Bud Light's parent company, demanding they halt the ads. This created a shitstorm of epic proportions.

During the legal process, Bud Light came under even more fire from the National Corn Growers Association, who put out press releases defending MillerCoors. A judge ruled in favor of MillerCoors and temporarily ordered Anheuser-Busch to stop using certain words affiliated with making beer and "corn syrup" in their ads.

This probably sounds like a PR nightmare. A lawsuit. Negative press releases from farmers. A pissed-off competitor with powerful allies. If you're like most business owners, you're probably cringing right now.

But Bud Light thought like a committed outlier and embraced the whole affair. They did something outrageously smart. Instead of admitting defeat, they claimed they won their lawsuit. After all, they were still allowed to run their attack ads, as long as they were more careful about the wording. They forged ahead.

Here's what's so rare and impressive about Bud Light. They embraced the fallout and ignored the "I'm offended by everything mob." That's smart, because that mob makes a lot of noise, but in reality, it represents very few agitated customers. Bud Light's ads resonated with their real target market, and they were wildly successful.

And guess what? It also takes a few days to remove a TV or radio ad and a few weeks to remove a billboard, so people probably still had the chance to see the ads even after the judge ordered them to be taken down.

Why is this a good thing, you ask? Because it was another bite of the apple when it came to branding Miller Lite and Coors Light as beers full of unhealthy corn syrup—and positioning themselves as the better choice. Hell, when I googled "miller lite corn syrup ad," a paid Google Ad appeared on the top of the search results with this:

Bud Light® | Brewed with No Corn Syrup | Hops. Barley. Water. Rice

Boom. That ad says it all. Bud Light is able to diminish Coors Light and Miller Lite's reputation without even using their names. Curious consumers who google the story will see that negative reinforcement. That's so damn smart.

This wasn't a 100% grand slam for Bud Light, but that wasn't their goal. Their goal was to gain market share and weaken the Coors Light and Miller Lite brands, and they did that with flying colors.

It was a carefully calculated risk, which meant it wasn't as risky as it may seem on paper. Bud Light spends more money on consumer data than most companies make in revenue every year. So they know exactly how to message and put a creative concept together. They know what a video should look like. They know the platforms to go to and the concept of the ad itself.

When Bud Light went after Miller Lite and Coors Light, they didn't do it because they thought, *Hmm...Let's figure something out. We need to get market share, so let's just accuse them of putting corn in their beer*. They did it because they saw it would be the "difference that would make a difference" when consumers were choosing between light beer options.

Remember, when you're defending against a comparatising ad, you're losing...and, no doubt, Coors Light and Miller Lite lost this round in the fight.

There's 1 other thing that propelled Bud Light forward during this campaign: those money-grubbing digital and traditional media complex members who exploited this conflict full tilt, just so they could get more clicks and views. By my estimate, it played into the millions of dollars in additional free publicity for Bud Light.

The media always loves a good fight, and Bud Light made sure they were the winners of that fight.

WHY YOU SHOULD USE THE MEDIA'S LOVE OF CONTROVERSY TO YOUR ADVANTAGE

I love companies that incorporate smart, authentic comparative advertising that serves 2 simultaneous purposes: endearing customers to the brand and crushing the competition. When a business can get a customer to laugh, build brand loyalty, and create negative feelings about their competition, that's a home run.

But we're just getting started, because if they can do that by running an ad campaign that creates a deep connection *and* gets a customer to freely give up their data, that's a grand slam.

I want to walk through a brilliant ad campaign that clearly utilized all the steps of the Undefeated Marketing System—but maybe not in the exact order. In this case, it's worth being the exception.

Enter Burger King. What did they do? They ran an 8-day marketing campaign that was easily one of the best I've seen in recent years. They ran a marketing campaign offering 1-cent Whoppers to the general public.

First, they built a connection with the public. 1-cent burgers equal happy customers.

Then, in order to get the 1-cent Whoppers, customers had to download the Burger King app. In essence, that meant that Burger King offered practically free food in exchange for their customers' data.

With all that willingly given data, Burger King was now able to study who these people were, understand what they cared about, and retarget those customers with ads in the future. Brilliant.

It gets even better, though. In order to actually get their Whopper, the customer had to order it from any McDonald's restaurant located less than 600 feet from a Burger King. Burger King literally taunted the competition by having its customers go to a McDonald's, order a Whopper, and then leave to go get their burger from Burger King. This campaign was named "The Whopper Detour," which made it even funnier and more memorable—the keys to a successful branding effort (Step 3).

By the way, are you offended that Burger King used comparatising against McDonald's? Of course not.

Burger King took creative comparatising to a whole new level. The only ones offended were McDonald's executives. Plus, Burger King got a buyer who willingly gave up their data. That is some marketing-inspired jujitsu. But because there's nothing the media likes more than conflict, there's another piece to this story.

The 8-day marketing ploy received millions of dollars in free advertising. Yes, the media put Burger King on a pedestal and dubbed McDonald's as the restaurant that got punk'd. Here are a few examples of the media throwing lighter fluid on the ad campaign:

- "Burger King trolls McDonald's with 1 cent burger promotion" (CNN)
- "Burger King is selling Whoppers for a penny—but you need to head to McDonald's first" (*USA Today*)
- "How to Get Burger King's 1-Cent Whoppers" (Yahoo)

I wouldn't be surprised if this pushed Burger King's earned media dollars into the 8-figure mark. Yes, over $10 million in *free* media. Unless you have the most innovative campaign known to human-kind, positive advertising will rarely get you that kind of free exposure. It's just a fact. The media loves a good controversy. You can use that to your advantage.

You don't always have to create the controversy. You just have to be ready to capitalize on it. Remember in Chapter 6 when I told you how leveraging media can help you build your brand? Sometimes you can also leverage media coverage about your competitors.

Think about it for a second. In that Midwestern gubernatorial race, we didn't break the story about our competitor's plagiarism. But we sure as hell capitalized on it.

That's also what the shoe company Skechers did when they launched an epic ad campaign against Nike. I was drawn to this story because it was similar to the comparatising ad that we created for 1 of our clients, which I mentioned earlier.

During a much-hyped, must-see college basketball game between Duke and North Carolina, something terrible happened. The game tipped off as planned, and seconds in, Duke's top player at the time, Zion Williamson, made a cut near the free-throw line. Then, out of nowhere, his shoe blew out and his knee buckled. Williamson was hurt and out of the game, meaning that college basketball's marquee star, on its biggest stage, was done in by shoe disintegration. That Nike shoe ended up losing Duke the game. Talk about a PR nightmare.

To Nike's credit, they quickly jumped on the situation and did an excellent job responding under terrible circumstances. But the real story is how smart one of their shoe rivals, Skechers, was in capitalizing on Nike's misfortune.

Skechers ran ads in the Sunday edition of the *New York Times*, the *Wall Street Journal*, *USA Today*, and the *Oregonian* (the newspaper of record in Nike's home state). The ads boldly proclaimed, "Just Blew It," next to a picture of a blown-out shoe where the rubber sole had pulled away from the nylon.

That campaign was genius because it was a play on Nike's famed marketing campaign of "Just Do It." It made people smile and gained Skechers millions of dollars in free advertising as news outlets all over the world ran the story. Plus, Skechers was able to indirectly promote its own basketball shoe (which, it was implied, never would have disintegrated on national television).

But that's not the only cool thing here. Skechers deserves credit for not falling in line with "groupthink" marketing by only advertising on social media / digital platforms. Instead, they ran the majority of this marketing campaign in hard copy, old-timey newspapers. I assume they did this because Skechers' brilliant marketing team followed their consumer data instead of automatically hopping online. They knew they would get online exposure when the ad went viral, so by targeting newspapers, they also maximized their ad spend. For the reduced price of buying print ads, they could get more free exposure.

Here's the bottom line: your marketing needs to cut through the noise. Generic content, nice videos, and easy messaging aren't going to stand out in a saturated market. It's just not as emotional or interesting. Point-blank.

If you really want to catch the media's attention and, by proxy, your customers' attention, the best way to do that is to create distinctions between your brand and others.

NEGATIVE ADVERTISING WILL GIVE YOU POSITIVE RESULTS

In a political or corporate marketing campaign, you must be on offense and be the one driving the conversation. Because when you create the narrative, you're in charge.

That's the principle that spurred us on in our campaign against the Midwestern gubernatorial plagiarizer. Our strategy immediately put the opponent on the defensive, and that allowed our candidate to take control of the debate.

Whether in politics or business, comparison ads work. If they're done right, they'll work far better than positive ads...*Every. Single. Damn. Time.*

That's why I'm so surprised at how resistant business owners are to the idea of comparatising. Look, you don't have to go supremely negative to make comparatising work for you. You don't have to offend any current or potential customers. You just have to be willing to go out on a limb, own your marketing, and set yourself apart from the competition. Your customers will appreciate you for your candor and uniqueness.

The bottom line? Comparatising *works*. But you have to use it with finesse, a certain flair, and creativity if you want to disrupt your market and more established competitors. Comparatising with this delicate formula will help brand your company to consumers as the underdog, attract fans that root for you, and yield big returns.

Drawing distinctions is the key to building stronger connections with your customers. (I'd highlight or write down that quote.) So take the chance and see bigger results.

CONCLUSION

THE LAST THING YOU WANT TO THINK ABOUT EVERY DAY is marketing. It's a pain in the ass, and it probably distracts you from the things you're really passionate about with your business. I get it.

But you also know it's a necessity, so you hire some experts and hope they'll do the job right. Unfortunately, most marketing agencies tell you to write big checks on Day 1. The fact that you don't want to think about marketing works in their favor because they know they can do the minimum work for maximum revenue.

As I revealed in *Fire Them Now*, your marketing agency is lying to you. They tell you that you have to sign a long-term contract. That you have to spend big money to know what works. That hourly rates are the way to go. That your ads should be all about your product or service. That they're working hard when, really, they're hardly working. That they care about your outcomes. And if you just brand it first, an infinite amount of customers will find you.

None of that is true.

You don't have to buy into those lies, and you certainly don't need to pump money into a marketing system that doesn't work. There's a better way to market your business. There's a secret formula that elects presidents and grows big and small businesses that you can follow to eliminate risk and ensure that your marketing dollars grow your company exponentially.

This formula has helped business owners all across the United States grow bigger and faster than they've ever grown before. This formula works, which is why it's called "the Undefeated Marketing System."

Whether you are a B2B or B2C business, if your outcome is to create genuine, lasting relationships with your customers and clients and exponentially grow your bottom line, this system will work for you.

The 5-step Undefeated Marketing System is the solution. *Every. Single. Time.*

When you dive deep and create a data-backed marketing campaign, you'll be able to understand the needs, wants, and desires of your customers, so you can eventually create raving fans faster than you ever thought possible. And one of the best parts of the Undefeated Marketing System is that it's easy to measure your success every step of the way. Once the 5-step system is well underway, you can stop spending so much time thinking about your marketing and get back to the parts of your business you really care about.

I'm sure you're thinking, *Implementing these 5 steps isn't as easy as Phillip is making them out to be.* I'll tell you in advance—you're right. The Undefeated Marketing System takes a lot of work. It's a big challenge that will sometimes go against your brain wiring, which always seeks the fast and easy route. Following the formula takes *commitment*, not *interest*. You have to see the process through.

But your business is worth it. It represents who you are. It represents your financial security, creating a better life for your family, and your ultimate legacy. So why would you cut corners when it comes to your marketing?

For those of you who are willing to commit and accept the challenge, it will pay off. You will have more success in your business, and you will beat the shit out of your competition. And before long, you'll be undefeated.

2 FREE GIFTS FOR YOU

1. Free Data Assessment of Your Customers/Clients

Throughout this book, you've heard a lot about the Customer Insights Report and how important customer data is for building lasting relationships with your customers. I've said it before, and I'll say it again: if you want to be undefeated, your first step is taking a deep dive into your customer or client data.

See for yourself just how much customer insights can help your business. My corporate marketing agency, Win BIG Media, is offering a free customer data assessment to help you find out how your ideal customers or clients think, feel, and act. We'll use our patented process to analyze your consumer data. Then we'll show you how those insights can help you connect with your customers and drive more conversions.

You can email me for the free data assessment at PS@phillipstutts.com or go to phillipstutts.com/insight to get started.

2. Free Marketing Audit of Your Business

In *Fire Them Now*, my corporate marketing agency offered readers a risk-free digital marketing audit of their company at no cost. Before that book was published, we performed this audit for our top clients at a cost of $5,000. We give a complete audit of your website, social media presence, platforms, and budget.

We want to help as many people as possible, so that offer still stands. We'll point out what you can improve so you can get a leg up on working your way through the Undefeated Marketing System.

If your business is already on track for undefeated success, we'll tell you that too. There's no obligation either. This marketing audit is our gift to you.

To take advantage of this limited-time offer, visit phillipstutts.com/audit.

If you're not quite ready to jump in (but seriously, why not?), you can also subscribe to my biweekly marketing insights email at phillipstutts.com. It's full of marketing ideas, consumer data, and future economic predictions to help your business thrive in any economy.

20 PROVEN TACTICS YOU SHOULD UTILIZE IN YOUR DATA-BACKED STRATEGY

FOR THOSE THAT DON'T HAVE THE MONEY TO INVEST IN the Undefeated Marketing System, that's okay. Implement your own version of the 5-step Undefeated Marketing System and employ these proven tactics in your data-backed strategy to take your marketing to the next level.

They come with a caveat, though. If you've already read this book, you know how hard I am on traditional marketers who play whack-a-mole with tactics. Here's the truth. I love tactics—as long as they're in line with your data-backed strategic marketing plan.

Before you put any of these 20 tactics into play, make sure they're aligned with your customer/client data and figure out how they factor into your strategic plan.

1. In all my years of marketing, there are 3 types of ads that I have consistently seen convert at a higher rate than any other types of ads: ads with 5-star reviews that offer social proof, humorous ads that create a connection with customers through laughter, and comparatising ads that effectively draw a distinction between a brand, product, or service and its competitors. So, if you're going to create an ad and want to stick to a tried-and-true template, I would choose 1 of those 3 types of ads.

2. Here's my favorite tactic of all time. If you want a cheap way to target interested customers and collect their data, run an ad on social media where you offer cash, merchandise, or a cool prize for people who share the post with friends and leave a positive comment. First, you will build a retargeting audience for free. Next, supersize your offer by asking these prospects to DM you their email address for 10 additional entries in the contest. Now you get the data away from the social platforms. Third, award the prize to anyone that sent you their email. Yes, all of them. It's cheap advertising, and you should also include a gift card for 10% off in the package of free merch you send them. You will now convert them into raving fan customers. (And it's likely that their first purchases will pay for the entire ad campaign, so it's virtually risk-free.) If your lifetime value is 2x or 10x, then you will make a ton of money over a customer's lifetime. Oh, one more thing. If you invest $500 to $1,000 into marketing the contest, you'll put this idea on steroids.

3. Have a 60-second video on your website featuring you, the business owner. Explain the story of your company, the

people who work there, and your mission. It should move quickly, and you can even toss in humor. I included a blooper reel at the end of my video, which you can see at winbigmedia. com. Again, it's all about the personal connection.

4. In Chapter 4, I talked about how much I appreciated the thank-you notes I received from Billy Reid and Guidry Organic Farms. Here's another story on the power of sending handwritten thank-you notes to your customers and clients. Flashback to November 2004. President George W. Bush had just won a second term as president, and I had just finished a 3-year political campaign run on his behalf, where I had 21 days off—*total*. It was a time of uncertainty and vulnerability because I was exhausted and knew I was about to start a new chapter in my life. And that's when President George W. Bush's top campaign advisor, Karl Rove, changed my life, helped me become a better person, and frankly, made me millions—*with 1 simple action*. I received a handwritten note from Rove thanking me for my service on behalf of the president. That thank-you note changed my life. The act was simple, it was generous, it was thoughtful...and I deeply appreciated it. *Why did Karl Rove do it?* It's easy really: he cared, he was grateful, and he was willing to carve out his most valuable asset—time—to express it. And so I did the same thing. I saw a small gesture like a handwritten thank-you note go 1,000 times further than an email "thank-you," a phone call "thank-you," or worse, the "thank-you" text. Write every customer a handwritten thank-you note after each purchase. This 1 tactic alone has helped make more meaningful connections with my clients, and those relationships have grown my business into the millions.

5. Nothing creates brand loyalty like recognition. Run a social media post recognizing your "Customer of the Week," and make the story about the customer, not your product or service. They will re-share it to all their friends and family. If you want to take the idea to the next level, you can also give them an exclusive discount code to share for winning the "award." This costs you nothing, and it rewards your loyal customers and creates referrals.

6. Cody Foster is the owner and founder of Advisors Excel, a financial services company, and he came up with a brilliant marketing tactic for B2B businesses. Advisors Excel's target clients are financial planners, and they created a "Wall of Fame" for any financial planner who sells over $100 million in Advisors Excel's financial products. The company flies the planner and their family out for an award ceremony and installs a bronze plaque in their honor. Here's why this is genius: it gives the financial planner a legacy, and it inspires every other financial planner to strive for the Wall of Fame. Advisors Excel has even been able to leverage some PR (e.g., newspaper and trade magazine articles) from the award because it has become prestigious among financial planners. Creating a Wall (or Hall) of Fame is a great way to honor your target client, create status and envy to motivate your other clients, and create raving fans. Just think about it: the people who make it onto the wall will never give their business to another company again. This tactic costs very little, but it's a very effective way to recognize your clients' achievements and make them into heroes.

7. If you want to build a raving fan base, always give your cus-

tomers and clients more than they expect. For example, when someone signs a contract with you or makes a purchase, send them a welcome package, free gift, or discount code. Give first to create loyalty.

8. Instead of using actors and models for your creative video, use real customers to tell an authentic, heartfelt story about themselves and your product or service. When the customer is the hero, you will always win.

9. When I lived in Washington, DC, life was expensive. There was a 9.85% city income tax, and private schools for my daughter were going to cost anywhere between $35,000 and $55,000 per year. Not to mention the high property taxes, utilities, and other necessary expenses. I added up the numbers and thought, *This just doesn't make sense. Over the next 20 years, it's going to cost me an extra $3 million just to live in DC.* So, in 2014, my wife and I moved to Florida, largely because the state had a major incentive: zero state income taxes. Clearly, we weren't the only ones drawn in by that incentive. People are leaving states with high taxes, like California, New York, and Massachusetts, in droves, and they're moving to states without income taxes, like Texas, Florida, and Tennessee. Here's the deal: incentives work. People are strongly motivated by the incentives they're offered. And that's not just true about where people want to live. For example, American Airlines recently sent me an email and said I could upgrade to platinum status for a small fee. Typically, it would cost a couple thousand dollars, but they were offering it to me for a couple hundred. They were clearly trying to find ways to incentivize their customers to invest more money in the company. And

you know what? When it comes to the overall lifetime value of those customers, those incentives will pay off.

10. Who do you hate more, politicians or lawyers? My vote goes to lawyers, and it's not even close. And who are the worst lawyers? It's gotta be those annoying charlatans on billboards, preying on the poor and vulnerable by marketing their services to sue anyone. But an Alabama real estate agent named Matt Curtis figured out a brilliant marketing tactic where he mocked those annoying lawyer billboards and grew his business (without spending much money). Matt copied the exact brand of one of the most notorious egomaniac lawyers and then used digital marketing to laugh, parody, and showcase his idea. It cost very little money, made people laugh, and ultimately, drew tons of attention for Matt's business. This is a perfect example of comparatising. You can steal Matt's idea and create your own billboard by duplicating the annoying lawyer in your community. Then you can draw attention to it by posting what you did and why on social media, and even consider spending some money to promote it. But remember, for this to resonate the same way, it has to be funny and natural. Bottom line? Find opportunities to have fun with your marketing and grow your business at the same time. Isn't that every entrepreneur's dream?

11. Try newsjacking, which means injecting your ideas into a breaking news story to generate tons of media coverage. If you want to make this concept a marketing science, buy the definitive book *Newsjacking*, by David Meerman Scott. For even more insights, I highly recommend Scott's other bestselling book about building raving fans, *Fanocracy*.

12. The actor Ryan Reynolds owned Aviation Gin, and he quickly gained a reputation for his humorous ads and promotional appearances. For example, when he revealed his Aviation Gin email address on the *Tonight Show Starring Jimmy Fallon*, the Aviation Gin server crashed after 20,000 emails flooded in. His snarky out-of-office replies were so popular, the company's computer servers crashed. A couple of years later, the company ended up selling for $600 million. There's an important lesson in this story: if you use a celebrity to market your business, don't just use them as a silent "face." Have them use humor and authenticity to give your target customers/clients a positive feeling about your company and generate profits.

13. One of our clients was a national executive-level job placement and recruitment firm looking to increase their brand awareness at a big conference at the MGM Grand in Las Vegas. We targeted the physical location of the hotel conference room and achieved a 275% increase in their daily website traffic and an 18% higher average click-through rate than the industry standard. To zero in on your target audience, target a physical location visited by your top buyers (e.g., a conference hotel).

14. Build an internal company culture that your customers, clients, and internal team feel and believe. One way we do that at my company is through the Big Personal Impact program. We show that we care by giving personalized gifts to our top clients, customers, and employees. Gift cards don't help you build relationships, but thoughtful outlier gifts are meaningful. For example, when one of our clients had a baby, we sent

her a monogrammed blanket with the baby's initials. When one of our team members had a grandparent in the hospital, we sent flowers with a personalized note telling the granddad how special the employee was to the company and how much he loved his granddad. Ask yourself, How can my business be less generic with our gestures?

15. Showcase your commitment to helping others. You can do this in 2 main ways. The first is to build a cultlike following by promoting your charity work. This has worked incredibly well for Chick-fil-A, who has made over $19 million in charitable and sponsorship donations over the past few years. They also give employees the opportunity to volunteer during working hours, and they're closed on Sunday. Besides their chicken sandwich, that overall commitment has put them on top. The second way is to give your customers the choice to help others. For example, when you offer a discount for your products or services, ask your customer, "Do you want the discount, or do you want to pay the full price and give the discounted amount to a charity of your choice?" Those last words are important. It should be a charity of *their* choice, not yours. Giving your customers the choice empowers them, makes them feel good, and makes them feel like you have a deep understanding of the causes they care about.

16. Doesn't it make sense that your customers'/clients' needs will change along with the economy? Make sure your marketing takes those changes into account. Over the years, we've learned that customers respond to "discounts" in a bad economy and language like "bundling" in a great economy. The latter makes them feel smart, rather than cheap.

17. When pitching a potential client or customer in person or via video conference call, always try to ask at least 3 questions that allow them to give you their opinions, wants, desires, needs, or feedback. I call this the "3-Tick Rule," because you should tick *a minimum* of 3 questions off your list during every interaction with them. Not only will this help you understand your potential customer or client better, but we have also observed that utilizing this tactic has given us a 75% higher close rate.

18. Use an email signature card with your picture on it. My email response rates have increased by over 50% because the people I email see a picture of me and know I'm real. Remember, marketing is all about forming personal connections.

19. Imagine that you had a business selling products on Amazon, and you spent years building a following. You had tons of 5-star reviews and repeat customers. Now, imagine that one day, Amazon suddenly decided to pull the plug on your shop. What would you do? If that was your only means of communicating with your customers, your business would be dead. I see so many business owners who let social media platforms and online retailers, like Amazon, completely control their customer data. That means they're essentially *renting* customers from those platforms. Don't rent your customers by relying solely on those platforms for storing your customer data. Do everything you can to collect information about your customers and connect with them outside of those platforms. For example, if you're selling products on Amazon, include a note in the package that says, "If you visit our website and sign up, we'll give you a 20% discount on your next purchase." Then, when they come back to you directly, you'll *own* that

data, and you'll have access to it, no matter what happens. Here's the bottom line: *you must collect and own your data.* When you own your customer or client data, you own your business.

20. How did I grow my political marketing agency, Go BIG Media, into an 8-figure business in 3 years without running a single ad? I followed the 3 Rs: reputation, relationships, and referrals. First of all, when I started the company, I had already worked in politics for more than 20 years, and I had a *reputation* for winning races. Second, I had built a number of solid *relationships* during those 20-plus years. And third, I used my reputation and relationships to earn *referrals* for my business. For example, we grew our business by partnering with another political media firm. They specialized in TV ads, while we specialized in digital advertising. So we were able to combine our networks and build a complementary partnership that produced millions of dollars in new business. If you can figure out those 3 things—reputation, relationships, and referrals—you may never have to run an ad *ever*. I certainly haven't.

ABOUT THE AUTHOR

PHILLIP STUTTS comes from the cutthroat world of political marketing. He has over 2 decades of experience working on campaigns with billions of dollars in political ad spend and has contributed to over 1,400 election victories, including 3 US presidential victories. Phillip plays the game of political and corporate marketing on the highest level, battling it out with fierce competition, multibillion-dollar budgets, and a win-or-die mentality.

He is the founder and CEO of Win BIG Media (a corporate marketing agency) and founder / executive chairman of Go BIG Media (a political marketing firm). Phillip is also the bestselling author of *Fire Them Now: The 7 Lies Digital Marketers Sell and the Truth about Political Strategies That Help Businesses Win*.

In addition to being represented by Gary Vaynerchuk's Vayner-Speakers, Phillip has made more than 350 national media appearances including CBS, ESPN, Fox News, Fox Business, MSNBC, and CNN. He has also been interviewed by renowned business, entertainment, and health leaders, including Gary Vaynerchuk, Peter Diamandis, James Altucher, Michael Hyatt, Jay Abraham, Adam Carolla, Dr. Drew Pinsky, and Dr. Steven Gundry.

Fox Business has lauded Phillip for creating "a marketing system that has generated record sales" for his clients and also described him as a "marketing genius." He's also been called "The Michael Jordan of Political Marketing" and "the political guru" by ESPN. You can contact Phillip at phillipstutts.com.

ABOUT PHILLIP STUTTS'S COMPANIES

Win BIG Media is a full-service, one-stop-shop corporate marketing agency that utilizes the 5-step Undefeated Marketing System to grow your business in any economy. With data at our core, Win BIG Media fully analyzes the real-time behavioral, emotional, and psychological characteristics of your target market to confidently build a winning strategy, design award-winning creative, video, and branding, and ultimately convert new customers and clients. You can reach the team at Win BIG Media here: winbigmedia.com.

Go BIG Media, Inc. is a political media and marketing firm that has received national acclaim for its work on behalf of US senators, governors, and presidential candidates. Notably, it has won over 45 awards for its excellence in political advertising, including a Pollie award from the American Association of Political Consultants for "Best Digital/Internet Independent Expenditure

Presidential Campaign" and a Peer Choice Award for "Digital Video Excellence in a Presidential Campaign." You can reach the team at Go BIG Media here: gobigmediainc.com.

Phillip Stutts & Company is an exclusive private consulting practice, where Phillip personally works with elite CEOs and C-suite marketing leaders to bring their business and marketing to the next level. You can book Phillip to speak and subscribe to his biweekly marketing insights email here: phillipstutts.com.

CPSIA information can be obtained
at www.ICGtesting.com
Printed in the USA
LVHW092339120421
684033LV00008B/1

9 781544 520155